DATE DUE

Demco, Inc. 38-293

Salman Rushdie

Twayne's English Authors Series

Kinley E. Roby, Editor

Northeastern University

TEAS 488

Salman Rushdie. *Photograph courtesy of CANAPRESS*

Salman Rushdie

by James Harrison

University of Guelph

Twayne Publishers • New York
Maxwell Macmillan Canada • Toronto
Maxwell Macmillan International •
New York   Oxford   Singapore   Sydney

Salman Rushdie
James Harrison

Copyright © 1992 by Twayne Publishers

Twayne Publishers   Maxwell Macmillan Canada, Inc.
Macmillan Publishing Company   1200 Eglinton Avenue East
866 Third Avenue   Suite 200
New York, New York 10022   Don Mills, Ontario M3C 3N1

Macmillan Publishing Company is part of the Maxwell Communication Group of
Companies.

Library of Congress Cataloging-in-Publication Data

Harrison, James, 1927-
    Salman Rushdie / by James Harrison.
        p.   cm. — (Twayne's English authors series ; TEAS 488)
    Includes bibliographical references (p. 142) and index.
    ISBN 0-8057-7011-9 (alk. paper)
    1. Rushdie, Salman.   2. Novelists, English—20th century-
-Bibliography.   3. Islam and literature.   4. India in literature.
I. Title.   II. Series.
823'.914—dc20
    [B]   91-30673
                                                CIP

10 9 8 7 6 5 4 3 2 1

Printed in the United States of America.

For Vivienne with love

Contents

Preface

> I would like to inform all the intrepid Muslims in the world that the author of the book entitled *The Satanic Verses,* which has been compiled, printed, and published in opposition to Islam, the Prophet, and the Qur'an, as well as those publishers who were aware of its contents, have been declared *madhur el dam* (i.e., "those whose blood must be shed"). I call on all zealous Muslims to execute them quickly, wherever they find them, so that no one will dare to insult Islam again. Whoever is killed in this path will be regarded as a martyr . . .
> —Ayatollah Khomeini, 14 February 1989

In these words the Ayatollah Khomeini's notorious *fatwa* against Salman Rushdie and his publishers was given to the world.[1] The sentence was pronounced without the trial which, according to Islamic law, should precede the putting into effect of any such fatwa or expression of legal opinion.[2] To reach the verdict the person sitting in judgment did not feel any obligation to read the offending document, *The Satanic Verses.* And that verdict has since been endorsed by millions of protesting Muslims in a state of equally uncontaminated ignorance.

Also unread by most of the Prophet Muhammad's detractors, from the Middle Ages to the nineteenth century, was the book of which he was, if not the author, then the sole human recipient—the Qur'an. What follows is Edward W. Said's account of the matter in his arresting study of Orientalism, the process whereby the Occident has created, as its own self-flattering antithesis in virtually all respects, the concept of the Orient.

They [figures of speech associated with the Orient] are all declarative and self-evident; the tense they use is the timeless eternal . . . [frequently] the simple copula *is.* Thus Mohammed[3] *is* an imposter, the very phrase canonized in d'Herbelot's *Bibliothèque* and dramatized in a sense by Dante. No background need be given; the evidence necessary to convict Mohammed is contained in the "is." One does not qualify the phrase, neither does it seem necessary to say that Mohammed *was* an imposter, nor need one consider for a moment that it may not be necessary to repeat the statement. It *is* repeated, he *is* an imposter, and each time one says it, he becomes more of an imposter and the author of the statement gains a little more authority in having declared it. Thus Humphrey Prideaux's famous seventeenth-century biography of Mohammed is subtitled *The True Nature of Imposture.*

Finally, of course, such categories as imposter (or Oriental, for that matter) imply, indeed require, an opposite that is neither fraudulently something else nor endlessly in need of explicit identification. And that opposite is "occidental," or in Mohammed's case, Jesus.[4]

It is small wonder that the Muslim response to *The Satanic Verses* has, again in Said's words, been: "Why must a Moslem, who could be defending and sympathetically interpreting us, now represent us so roughly, so expertly, and so disrespectfully to an audience already primed to excoriate our traditions, reality, history, religion, language, and origin? Why, in other words, must a member of our culture join the legions of Orientalists in Orientalizing Islam so radically and so unfairly?"[5]

Said himself, of course, sees *The Satanic Verses* as "an astonishingly and prodigiously inventive work of fiction" by "the same distinguished writer and intellectual who has spoken out for immigrants', black, and Palestinian rights," and he describes the threat to Rushdie's life as "the ghastly violence prescribed by Ayatollah Khomeini." He knows, nonetheless, that "what shocks Moslems in the novel is the book's knowing intimacy with the religious and cultural material it so comically and resourcefully plays with."[6]

It is no major part of my objective in this study to reach conclusions as to the rights and wrongs of the quarrel between Rushdie and the Muslim world. I came to his earlier novels via spending a boyhood in Sri Lanka and India, writing a Twayne monograph on Kipling, and teaching a graduate course on novels about India, from *Kim* and *A Passage to India* to *Midnight's Children* and *Clear Light of Day*. I wrote an article on *Midnight's Children* and *Shame* before *The Satanic Verses* was published, and it had been accepted before the whole subject hit the headlines. So in many ways the Ayatollah has complicated what was a fairly simple love-at-first-sight relationship between a reader and an author's work. Yet in other ways, since I have obviously not been able to ignore it, Khomeini's intervention has clarified matters, highlighting the central issue in *The Satanic Verses* and making it stand out amid the usual Rushdie *embarras de richesses* in a way that otherwise might not have been possible. This much at least I feel I must say at the outset: on the one hand, no government should be able to put out contracts on the citizens of other nations with impunity; on the other, we in the West need to remember for how long and how much more often we have at least equally contemptuously denied the humanity of those "lesser breeds without the law," to use Rudyard Kipling's phrase, who are now asserting their rights. Murder is no more justified by a threat to the profits of corporations than by a slur on the Prophet of Islam.

As for the clash of values involved, between the right to speak and write freely and the obligation to respect other people's most treasured beliefs, we may have to recognize that in this as in other instances no compromise that will satisfy everyone is possible. Does one give the child of Jehovah's Witnesses a blood transfusion and in saving his or her life call forth the parents' deepest feelings of revulsion, or does one let the child die? Do we insist on Rushdie's right to say what, with a sincerity fierce enough to override considerations that would deter most of us, he is convinced needs saying? Or do we respect the fierce protectiveness toward their faith of people belonging to a culture that regards freedom of speech as trivial compared with the honor of the founder of that faith?

Clearly I shall find myself returning periodically to the social and political repercussions of all of Rushdie's work and of *The Satanic Verses* in particular. That is entirely as it should be, since Rushdie is insistent, in his essay "Outside the Whale"[7] and elsewhere, that literature cannot avoid having a political component. Rushdie's concern is to call attention to the way the literary themes of novels and plays reflect and in their turn affect social and political structures. My concern is to show how the social and political themes of Rushdie's novels enter into and help to shape their purely literary structures. Ultimately I hope to demonstrate, however, that all such aspects of his output make up an indivisible whole.

Acknowledgments

My thanks are due first and foremost to Salman Rushdie, not merely for the fascinating primary sources he has provided me with for a study but also for his courtesy and encouragement in replying to my queries. I am indebted to the librarians at the University of Guelph as always for their help, to my editors for their advice and trust, and to my colleagues Douglas Killam, Diana Brydon, and Patrick Holland for their encouragement and support. I am especially grateful to Patrick Holland for reading the entire manuscript with his usual close attention and to Justin MacGregor, the graduate student with whom a weekly exchange of ideas on Rushdie was always stimulating. I owe much to many, but the final responsibility, especially for any mistakes, is mine. Finally I thank my wife, Vivienne, the sine qua non of it all.

Parts of chapters 4 and 5 first appeared in my article "Reconstructing *Midnight's Children* and *Shame*," published in the *University of Toronto Quarterly,* to whose editors I am indebted.

My thanks are also due to Victor Gallancz, Ltd., and the Overlook Press for permission to quote from *Grimus;* to Jonathan Cape, Ltd., and Alfred A. Knopf, Inc., for permission to quote from *Midnight's Children* and *Shame;* to Penguin Books, Ltd., London, Viking Penguin, Inc., New York, and Penguin Books Canada, Ltd., for permission to quote from *The Satanic Verses;* to Aitken and Stone, Ltd., and Salman Rushdie for permission to quote from *In Good Faith;* and to Chatto and Windus, Ltd., for permission to quote from Malise Ruthven's *A Satanic Affair.*

Chronology

1947   Born in Bombay.

1954   Attends Cathedral School, Bombay.

1961   Sent to Rugby School in England.

1964   The family moves to Karachi in Pakistan, where Rushdie henceforward spends the school vacations.

1965–1968   Studies History at King's College, Cambridge.

1968–1969   Works as an actor at the Oval House, an experimental theater.

1969–1981   Works on and off, sometimes part-time, as a copywriter in advertising agencies, while he writes an unpublished novel, then *Grimus,* and finally *Midnight's Children.*

1974   Pays a five-month visit to Pakistan and India, preparatory to writing *Midnight's Children.*

1975   *Grimus.*

1976   Marries Clarissa Luard.

1981   *Midnight's Children,* for which he is awarded the Booker McConnell Prize for Fiction and the literary award from the English-Speaking Union.

1982   Awarded the James Tait Black Memorial Prize for *Midnight's Children.*

1983   *Shame.*

1986   Invited to visit Nicaragua.

1987   *The Jaguar Smile.*

1988   Marries American novelist Marianne Wiggins. *The Satanic Verses* is published in Britain; a copy is burned at a public protest by Muslims in Bradford; its sale is banned in India, Pakistan, South Africa, Saudi Arabia, and other Arab states.

1989   American edition of *The Satanic Verses,* followed by the issue of a fatwa (a legal ruling by the Ayatollah Khomeini) that Rushdie's offenses and those of his publishers are deserving of death, the offer of a monetary reward to any Muslim who kills Rushdie, and demands by Muslims throughout the world that publication of the book cease and its sale be banned. Rushdie is placed under police protection, constantly guarded, and frequently moved from one location to another.

1990   *Haroun and the Sea of Stories.*

1991   *Imaginary Homelands: Essays and Criticism.*

Salman Rushdie

Twayne's English Authors Series

Chapter One

Biography

Childhood and Education

Salman Rushdie was born in June 1947, two months before the simultaneous births of Saleem Sinai, the narrator and protagonist of *Midnight's Children,* and the newly independent states of India and Pakistan. Like Saleem,
Rushdie was born and grew up in Bombay; like Saleem, he led a protected,
middle-class life, was educated in English at the Cathedral Boys' High
School, and grew up a bilingual speaker of Urdu and English. Rushdie himself claims that, unlike Saleem's, his childhood was "uneventfully happy"
rather than "tempestuous and disturbed."[1] Other sources claim, however,
that as with Saladin Chamcha and his father in *The Satanic Verses* the relationship between Rushdie and his own father "was often stormy."[2] Be that
as it may, his Muslim family eventually decided to move to Pakistan, as did
Saleem's, and in 1964 they settled in Karachi. Three years earlier, however,
Rushdie had been sent to England to continue his education at Rugby
School, so it was only during the vacations that he lived in Pakistan.

One of the more prestigious public schools of England, Rugby claims as
its most famous headmaster Thomas Arnold, father of Matthew Arnold
and prime advocate of the earnest Victorianism that saw it as its duty to
"civilize" such "uncouth" cultures as were to be found in India. The school
that Dr. Arnold took over, and his struggles to civilize the barbaric culture
to be found there, are described graphically in Thomas Hughes's novel *Tom
Brown's Schooldays.* In *The Satanic Verses,* Rushdie describes some of his
own experiences at the present-day Rugby School. Elsewhere he has specu-
lated that, if only he had been any good at games, he would not have been
subjected so often to racial taunts from his peers. He has also said that being
taught in classes of six or seven students is an advantage that makes up for
much else and that life was better in his later years at school.[3] Nevertheless,
on graduating from Rugby he was reluctant to continue his education at
King's College, his father's alma mater at Cambridge, and finally agreed to
study history there only so as not to disappoint his parents.

Life at Cambridge he found to be utterly different from that at Rugby. In
his own words, "Public schools are basically composed of philistines. It was

an exciting time to be at Cambridge, from 1965 to 1968: it was a very politicized period. There was the Vietnam war to protest about, student power to insist upon, drugs to smoke, flowers to put in your hair, good music to listen to. It was a good time to be young, and I'm very pleased to have had those years: there was an energy about student life then."[4] While at Cambridge he wrote, among other things, a paper on "Muhammad, Islam, and the Rise of the Caliph" for part 2 of his history tripos.[5]

After Cambridge he worked for a while as an actor at the Oval House, a home for experimental theater of a variety of kinds and a meeting place for many of those "who are now mainstays of the British theatre."[6] What it was possible to earn there, however, was scarcely enough to live on, so he became a copywriter for an advertising agency. Eventually he was able to strike a deal whereby he worked for his employers for two or three days a week and himself for the remaining four or five. In this way he was able to write an unpublished apprentice novel, the early and unsuccessful *Grimus,* and *Midnight's Children.* As Rushdie puts it: "I thought of it as industrial sponsorship." He goes on to claim that it is possible to write commercials that do not tell lies and that he cannot remember writing anything that he did not think was true. But he admits that the people for whom you work in such a line of business "make you feel suspicious of what you are doing." So when he had finished writing *Midnight's Children,* but before it was published, he also stopped writing advertisements.[7]

Midnight's Children and *Shame*

Fortunately the novel was a runaway success, winning Britain's most prestigious literary award, the Booker McConnell Prize, as well as the James Tait Black Memorial Prize and the English-Speaking Union Literary Award. More importantly for the security it gave him as a writer, within three years it had sold a quarter of a million copies and had been translated into twelve languages. Rushdie had arrived.

One of the more interesting questions raised by the novel is that of Rushdie's nationality. Educated largely in England, choosing to live in England and to write in English, and by the time of its publication being a naturalized British citizen, he was suddenly best known as the author of a novel set in India and Pakistan. Indeed, *Midnight's Children* is the best-known novel about India written in English since *A Passage to India,* perhaps since *Kim,* and certainly the best-known novel ever written by an Indian. Such a claim implies that, whatever his passport says, Rushdie will always in some respects be an Indian—a fact that is unimportant in terms of the color of his skin but very important in determining the different angle from which he is able to view things.

Rushdie is one of an increasing band of writers who live as exiles from their native lands—by choice in cases such as those of V. S. Naipaul and Bharati Mukherjee and of necessity (until very recently) in those of Milan Kundera, Joseph Brodsky, Aleksandr Solzhenitsyn, and Josef Skvorecky. There have been such transplants in the past, of course—Henry James, T. S. Eliot, and W. H. Auden not needing to change language, Samuel Beckett writing in French and translating himself into English with equal facility, and Joseph Conrad wrestling with what was his third and for many years his least-familiar tongue. But it used to be axiomatic that the voluntary exile would either escape from his roots in order to be free to write about them, like James Joyce, or strike new roots like Conrad. Recently, however, a writer like Naipaul has been able to make a virtue of his rootlessness, writing fiction set in the Caribbean, London, or central Africa with apparently equal facility. Rushdie, by setting his second and third novels in India and Pakistan and only presuming to use England (his home for much longer than India and Pakistan combined) as the location for most of the action of his fourth, has clearly not achieved Naipaul's degree of detachment and may never do so. What is also clear, however, is that he is not exclusively—nor even, perhaps, primarily—an Indian novelist.

Such ambivalence is probably most obvious in his choice of English as the language in which to write. There are those, of course, who would argue that to use any language other than his or her native Urdu, Hindi, Bengali, Tamil, Gujarati, or whatever, disqualifies any Indian from being a truly Indian author. But many distinguished authors who are indisputably Indian, from Rabindranath Tagore and R. K. Narayan to Raja Rao and Anita Desai, have chosen to use English in some, most, or all of their writing. And there are good reasons for their having done so. Chinua Achebe has claimed to use English in his novels not primarily to reach the rest of the world outside Nigeria but to reach the whole of Nigeria.[8] And the same argument must apply with at least equal force to Narayan, whose native language of Tamil is spoken by no more than 15 or 16 percent of his fellow Indians. Rushdie, too, by writing in English rather than Urdu, has been able to reach a wider readership in India and Pakistan, though it would be disingenuous to deny that he has thereby also gained an enormously greater readership in the rest of the world. But an important and interesting reason Rushdie himself gives for preferring to write in English is that the language is so much more flexibly capable than Urdu of handling life in the twentieth century.[9] This flexibility is partly because English is used throughout the world by so many different societies and for so many different purposes. By contrast, few if any internationally known experts in economics, genetic engineering, jazz, nuclear physics, or psychology use Urdu as their chosen medium of communication. Far more importantly from Rushdie's point of view, however, few if any novels dealing with twentieth-century life and developing literary techniques equal to capturing its essence have been written in Urdu. As is very clearly implied by Anita Desai in her novels *Clear Light of Day* and *In Custody,* Urdu is a language that compels those who write in it to do so almost as if trying to write a novel in Latin.

Obviously, however, Rushdie's success depends on far more than simply choosing to write in English. What became very clear with the publication of *Midnight's Children* is that, of those Indian authors using English, Rushdie is by far the most innovatively confident stylist. Of his predecessors, moreover, probably only G. V. Desani in *All about H. Hatterr* was willing to handle language with anything approaching Rushdie's disrespectful relish and verve and, ultimately, respect. Such confidence is obviously in part a matter of temperament. But in Rushdie's case it is also the result of the displacement of Urdu by English as his first language long before he faced the question of which language to use in his writing.[10] Just living most of his life in a community where everyone around him manipulates the language with a modicum of the confidence and carelessly creative irreverence shown by Rushdie in his fiction is what has enabled him to feel so thoroughly at ease in the language. There is no need, therefore, for him to demonstrate that he can use it as correctly as if it were his mother tongue. Paradoxically, moreover, one of the most attractive results of his choice to write in English is that he is better able than other Indian writers to enrich his prose with features of syntax and vocabulary that are peculiar to Indian speakers of English. In this he resembles writers from the Caribbean, Australia, or Nigeria who feel free to lace their use of English with the local spirit.

It is probably this linguistic distance that more than anything else leads Rushdie to dissociate himself from any "school of Indian-British fiction." He claims, indeed, that "*Midnight's Children* was partly conceived as an opportunity to break away from the manner in which India had been written about in English, not just by Indian writers but by Western writers as well." And it is at this point in the interview that he acknowledges enjoying the way Desani showed him "that it was possible to break up the language and put it back together in a different way."[11]

Midnight's Children had been five years in the writing; *Shame* was published just two years later. It is a much shorter novel, but it was also an easier one to write. With both novels Rushdie wrote a first draft and followed this with a radically revised second one. In the case of *Midnight's Children* the second draft was embarked on to explore the largely unforeseen potential of a new approach. With *Shame,* however, the revision was undertaken in order to achieve a much more predetermined, specific effect. It is a novel with as close to a single satiric purpose—almost a single target—as Rushdie is ever likely to achieve or want to achieve. As a satire of the two figures who have dominated Pakistani politics since the defection of Bangladesh, the book won him few friends in high places in that country, its sale being officially banned.

Journalism and Politics

Rushdie's fiction may have restricted itself, in *Midnight's Children* and *Shame,* to the politics of the Indian subcontinent. But in his journalism, in articles such as "The New Empire within Britain," "She [Margaret Thatcher] Has Persuaded the Nation That Everything Which Goes Wrong Is an Act of God," and "The Council [subsidized] Housing That Kills,"[12] he is clearly concerned with contemporary political issues in Britain such as the problems faced by new immigrants from Commonwealth countries in Asia, Africa, and the Caribbean or by the poor in general who must rely on subsidized housing. Equally clearly, he is not in sympathy with Mrs. Thatcher's handling of those issues, any more than he supported her policy regarding the Falkland (or Malvinas) Islands.

There are those who find—in his wealthy middle-class Indian family background, his upper-class English education, his very English accent, and even his pale skin—too many barriers to his really understanding or representing the underprivileged, whether from the third or the first world.[13] The issue is of more concern in his novels, particularly *The Satanic Verses,* and is discussed later. But the evidence from his journalism indicates a degree of concern that, though exceeding his first-hand knowledge, is nevertheless genuine.

Most attractive of all to liberals is the extended piece of journalism Rushdie published as a book under the title *The Jaguar Smile* in 1987. Rushdie had taken a break from writing *The Satanic Verses* the year before and had visited Nicaragua as a guest of the Sandinista Association of Cultural Workers. This visit took place shortly after "the International Court of Justice in the Hague had ruled that US aid to *la Contra,* the counterrevolutionary army the CIA had invented, assembled, organized, and armed, was in violation of international law."[14]

As is clear from even that brief quotation, supporters of the Reagan policy concerning Nicaragua will find little in the book with which to agree. Yet Rushdie is quite severe in his criticism of his hosts over the closure of the opposition newspaper, *La Prensa,* and is not by any means ready to accept, either face to face or in his subsequent written account, all the justifications they put forward for that and other questionable policies. He is honest, too, about how badly served Nicaraguans are by their government-controlled media and consequently how ill-informed they are about the rest of the world. He reports that, listening to him and a visiting Russian novelist discuss *The Gulag Archipelago,* Nicaraguan writers present were incredulous at what they were hearing. How could such things be (99–100)? Nevertheless, as one born in a nation that had thrown off the British yoke, Rushdie's natural sympathies lay with the Nicaraguans. He found that he actually liked and admired the members of the government he met as human beings. "For the first time in my life," he writes, "I realized with surprise, I had come across a government I could support, not *faute de mieux,* but because I wanted its efforts (at survival, at building the nation, and at transforming it) to succeed" (70).

Almost in conclusion he analyzes the limerick he uses as epigraph and from which he takes his title.

> There was a young girl of Nic'ragua
> Who smiled as she rode on a jaguar.
> They returned from the ride
> With the young girl inside
> And the smile on the face of the jaguar.

How is one to read the parable? he asks. "If the young girl was taken to be the revolution, seven years old, fresh, still full of the idealism of youth, then the jaguar was geopolitics, or the United States; after all, an attempt to create a free country where there had been, for half a century, a colonized 'back yard,' and to do so when you were weak and the enemy close to omnipotent, was indeed to ride a jaguar. That was the 'leftist' interpretation; but what if the young girl were Nicaragua itself, and the jaguar was the revolution?" In the end he enigmatically chooses between "the two girls on the two jaguars. I tore up the picture which looked, well, *wrong,* and threw it away. In the one I preserved, the girl on the jaguar looked like the Mona Lisa, smiling her Gioconda smile" (161).

The Jaguar Smile bears the dedication "For Robbie," a reminder of the breakup of Rushdie's first marriage to Clarissa Luard, which is in some ways comparable to that between Saladin Chamcha and Pamela Lovelace in *The Satanic Verses*. On an extended visit to Australia Rushdie became passionately involved with Robyn Davidson in a relationship that some have seen as the equivalent of that between Gibreel Farishta and Alleluia Cone—also in *The Satanic Verses*. Before the book's publication, however, and in time for it to be dedicated to her and for her to share the first few months of what appeared to be a life sentence of police protection, Rushdie married the American novelist Marianne Wiggins.

Satan and the Ayatollah

Somebody in every sizable community in the world must know, by now, that the Ayatollah Khomeini condemned Salman Rushdie to death for writing *The Satanic Verses*. Setting aside for the moment such technical questions as what precisely the Ayatollah did or what he had the authority to do, it is important for the non-Islamic world to recognize that, to the extent Khomeini himself played any part in the book's rejection, his was a very late entry on the stage. The book was published in Britain on 26 September 1988. On 5 October its sale was banned in India by a government acutely aware of the electoral importance of the country's hundred million Muslims and under pressure from extremists alerted to the nature of the book by an interview with Rushdie in *India Today*.[15] On 24 November it was banned in South Africa, Rushdie having had to cancel a planned promotional tour of the country when the promoters felt unable to guarantee his safety from indignant Muslims in the Indian sector of the population. Within weeks, moreover, it was also banned in the predominantly Muslim states of Pakistan, Saudi Arabia, Egypt, Somalia, Bangladesh, Sudan, Malaysia, Indonesia, and Qatar.[16]

In the new year the book was ceremonially burned on 14 January during a demonstration in Bradford, a city in the north of England with a Pakistani minority that in certain areas constitutes a local majority. This protest was followed on 27 January by a demonstration in Hyde Park, London, and the presentation of a petition to Penguin. On 12 February there was a riot in Islamabad, Pakistan, where a crowd tried to storm the American embassy (publication date for the United States having been fixed for 15 February), and the police on guard killed five people and injured more than a hundred in defending the embassy. Then the very next day another person was killed and another hundred injured in similar riots in Kashmir.

Even the demonstrations in Britain were to some extent stage-managed by the leaders of Muslim organizations who were in a position to know enough about the book to influence their less-informed compatriots. Muslims have on the whole proved more reluctant to integrate and become part of Western societies than most other immigrants, in part because of their fear of losing their strong religious identity. From the start it has been the fundamentalist religious leaders, rather than the more liberal, Western-influenced intellectuals, who have been best able to respond to and exploit the Rushdie affair. They are the ones who have orchestrated the nevertheless very real resentment that Muslims have felt worldwide—but earliest and above all in the beleaguered Muslim communities of cities like Bradford —at the insulting treatment they feel their religion has received at Western (and now at at Westernized Eastern) hands. It is a sad irony that Rushdie has probably done far more to strengthen than to weaken those reactionary elements in Islam to which he is most opposed.[17]

In the case of the Pakistani riot, the organizers were almost certainly members of the Jamaat-i-Islam party, who were bitterly opposed to Benazir Bhutto as prime minister on the grounds that an Islamic state cannot be ruled by a woman and who were therefore glad of any opportunity to fan Islamic fervor. It also seems certain that the Ayatollah's fatwa of 14 February against Rushdie and his publisher—whether or not it was prompted by the fatal riots of the preceding two days and whether or not it was in response to a request from British Muslims for a legal ruling on Rushdie's guilt or innocence according to Islamic law—was influenced by the political situation in Iran. Clearly Khomeini did not have long to live. A power struggle between moderates and extremists was already taking place. Also, the end of a long war with Iraq had just removed a convenient scapegoat for all that was wrong with the country's economy and seemed to be the possible forerunner of other more moderate policies. So the extremists, feeling their hammer-lock on the nation slipping, lost no opportunity to "draw the Old Man's attention to any departures from the strict puritanism that had been the hallmark of his long and exemplary life."[18] What better opportunity than the publication of *The Satanic Verses* in the United States, "the Great Satan," to persuade Khomeini to give perhaps his last clarion call to the faithful and elicit new expressions of their devotion not just in Iran but throughout the world?

Another issue altogether is whether Khomeini exceeded his authority in his various pronouncements; there are several arguments that strongly suggest that he did. First, as a *mujtahid* (i.e., a Shia Muslim interpreter of the law—the equivalent of a Sunni Muslim *mufti*) he was only one of a number of Muslim authorities entitled to make a legal ruling on a point of law when asked to do so. Another jurist might well have given a different ruling; those asking the question went to the person most likely to give them the answer they wanted. Second, as one man's opinion, the fatwa and its recommendations should not have been put into effect until confirmed by a trial held according to proper procedures. Indeed, it is highly irregular for a fatwa to be issued at all on a matter occurring in the *Dar al-Harb* (i.e., territories where Muslim law does not operate) as opposed to the *Dar al-Islam.* Third, though a mujtahid can pronounce on a person's earthly guilt and appropriate punishment, only God can decide whether or not to accept the offender's repentance and exempt him or her from eternal damnation.[19] Yet Khomeini is reported as responding as follows to Rushdie's carefully phrased apology: "Even if Salman Rushdie repents and becomes the most pious man of time, it is incumbent on every Muslim to employ everything he has got, his life and his wealth, to send him to hell."[20] Last of all, to regard apostasy as a capital offense, especially when the apostate claims not to have practiced the religion as an adult, seems gratuitously barbaric.

None of the political factors complicating the situation should be allowed to obscure the fact, however, that the Muslim rank and file were genuinely shocked, deeply offended, and greatly angered by what they saw as an affront to their religion. More than that, Rushdie's book was a personal affront to the solitary Islamic equivalent to Christ, Mary, and all the saints, or to the entire pantheon of Hindu gods, those anthropomorphically approachable embodiments of differing aspects of Brahman, "the One that is the All." Divine revelations to Muslims begin and end with those granted to Muhammad. The only prophets preceding him are Jewish, and there have been none since, the Qur'an being considered as Allah's last word on everything. As a result, therefore, the Prophet Muhammad is the unique, revered, and rather lonely human element in a religion as uncompromisingly monotheistic as Judaism.

Until very recently, life for Rushdie since the Ayatollah's fatwa has been very much a closed book so far as the rest of the world is concerned. He has been under constant police protection and has been moved frequently; he has been able to phone friends though they cannot phone him; and he has received fairly regular visits from fellow writers and publishers. His wife, Marianne Wiggins, shared the first few months of his itinerant incarceration, but he has recently acknowledged, to no one's great surprise, that his "marriage is over."[21] The one human relationship he has been able to maintain throughout this ordeal has been with his son, Zafar, whom he phones daily, for whom he has written and to whom he has dedicated *Haroun and the Sea of Stories,* and who reviewed it (not enough "jump"[22]) in an early draft.

The story was apparently begun as a "bath-time" serial,[23] which Rushdie promised to write down one day. It was begun, that is, when the Ayatollah was a cloud no bigger than a man's hand. So apropos is its theme, however, given Rushdie's present situation, that the parallels cannot be unintended. For Haroun's father, Rashid Khalifa, is a master storyteller, the source of whose tales ("the Sea of Stories") has been contaminated by Khattam-Shud, "the Prince of Silence and the Foe of Speech." Luckily for Rashid, however, his son manages to get himself to Kahani, earth's second, invisible moon and location of the Sea of Stories, to engineer the overthrow of Khattam-Shud and his whole regime of silence and darkness and to ensure a happy ending to the story of his father's loss of storytelling magic.

Despite the immediate resemblance of Rashid's predicament and name to those of Rushdie, however, the story derives much of its quality and richness from features that have always been characteristic of Rushdie's work. There is a continual play of language, as in the Plentimaw Fish (in the Sea of Stories, of course) who ingest, digest, and then retell in new forms and combinations the sea's innumerable streams of story through their plentiful maws or mouths. Then there are the many P2C2Es (i.e., processes too complicated to explain) by means of which the Eggheads control the affairs of Kahani and the Land of Gup. But behind the playfulness is an implicit comment, insightful or satiric, on the processes of artistic creation and the ways of bureaucratic expertise. The whole success of Khattam-Shud, moreover, in establishing an oppressive regime of silence in the Land of Chup results from the prior success of the Eggheads in controlling (by an inevitable P2C2E) the rotation of Kahani so as to ensure perpetual day for the Gupees in Gup and consequent perpetual night for the Chupwalas in Chup. (Rushdie even pushes this dangerous and discriminatory dichotomization to such an extreme that certain Chupwalas and their shadows set up entirely separate existences.) Not surprisingly, therefore, Haroun achieves the overthrow of this silent wintry darkness by reestablishing a rotation for Kahani that ensures equal distribution of day and night for both Gupees and Chupwalas. And even the Eggheads applaud the wisdom of such a measure.

Yet never, as one reads the book, does such potential didactism displace, or overshadow, or even diminish the pleasure one derives from the playful inventiveness of the fantasy and the sheer vigor and "jump" of the story. It is as if the detailed ingenuity of *Grimus*'s science fiction and the nonchalant audacity of *Midnight's Children*'s magic realism have been combined to perfection.

One wishes that a similar reconciliation and happy ending to the story

were in sight for Rushdie himself. At the time I write he has made over-
tures to Muslim leaders in Britain and to certain more liberal Islamic theo-
logians in Egypt. He declares himself to be a Moslem who has regained his
faith; he disavows "any statement in my novel *The Satanic Verses* uttered
by any of the characters who insults the prophet Mohammed, or casts as-
persions upon Islam, or upon the authenticity of the holy Koran, or who
rejects the divinity of Allah," dismissing them as the dreams of a character
in the process of being destroyed by his loss of faith; and he undertakes not
to allow any paperback edition or further translations of the novel to
appear.[24] Such concessions appear to have met with cautious approval by
some Muslim leaders. But in Iran the Ayatollah Khomeini's successor has
reiterated his predecessor's rejection of any conceivable apology or repentance on the part of Rushdie and has continued to refuse to rescind the
death sentence.

Some of Rushdie's staunchest erstwhile supporters have been shocked by
what they see as a betrayal and have expressed disbelief, sorrow, even indignation at the thought of their favorite martyr turning lapsed skeptic. It
would seem impertinent to express an opinion on any decision he makes in
relation to his role as a pawn in the essentially political struggle between
moderates and extremists for control of Islam—a struggle taking place not
just in Iran but worldwide, with almost no one daring to be seen as other
than "politically correct," Muslim style, on the by now irrelevant fate of
Salman Rushdie. One holds one's breath for him and tries to refrain from
comment that might inflame the issue. But it is hard to foresee a time when
he will be subject to no more than the routine perils of a car accident or cancer of the lung.

Chapter Two
History, Religion, and Politics in India

One of the most interesting of the many comments made by Salman Rushdie on his own work forms part of an interview published in *Quinzaine littéraire* in 1985.

Finally, you need a special style to speak or write about India. The first thing you notice about the country, apart from the sheer number of people living there, is that they believe in God, that the divine is a part of everyday life. If you employ realism—a rational, Western way of using language—to describe such a society, you are implicitly being critical of it. Therefore you must use language in a manner which permits God to exist—the divine to be as real as the divan I am sitting on. In any case, realism can no longer express or account for the absurd reality of the world we live in—a world which has the capability of destroying itself at any moment.[1]

The sad irony of Rushdie's claim to use language so as to "permit God to exist" is, of course, that this is precisely what may result in Rushdie's not being permitted to continue to exist. There are strict regulations, it seems, as to the form in which God can be permitted to exist. What I wish to emphasize, however, is not the applicability of Rushdie's remarks to his own circumstances but their relevance to the whole of Indian history, culture, and literature. It is impossible to consider Indian history apart from religion—a comment that might well have been made of European history prior to the eighteenth century. But it is also impossible to consider Indian religious belief apart from Indian history, so integrally is each a part of the other.

Historical Background

India is often referred to as a subcontinent, a description that calls attention to both its size and its self-contained quality. The population of India, Pakistan, and Bangladesh totals more than 90 percent that of Europe (including European Russia) and 250 percent that of North and Central America, while seven of its languages (as compared with eight European languages) are among the twenty-one most widely spoken in the world, though its area is less than a sixth that of North America. Roughly half that area consists of a peninsula jutting into the ocean, and the other half forms a blunt wedge thrusting northward into Asia, its frontiers running along almost unbroken ranges of some of the highest mountains in the world. Only in the northwest, through the Khyber Pass from Afghanistan or the Bolan Pass from Persia (Iran), has it proved practicable to march into India with an army of any size. From that direction, however, have come many invasions, with the result that, for good or ill, winds of change in India have usually blown from the north. From the northwest came the founders of the Harappa culture, whose cities flourished in the Indus Valley circa 2300 B.C. Through the passes from central Asia came the Aryans in about 1500 B.C., whose interaction with more indigenous inhabitants of the subcontinent was to shape the future of Indian culture so decisively. Fresh from his conquest of Persia came Alexander of Macedon in 327 B.C., but he stayed for too short a time to leave a legacy of lasting importance. Shortly after this incursion the Maurya dynasty, whose Magadha Kingdom lay farther to the east in the Ganges Basin, began a series of campaigns that established a single empire throughout virtually the whole subcontinent for a century and a half or more. This dynasty left behind a nostalgic memory of greatness that would not be recaptured until the Mughal Empire of the sixteenth and seventeenth centuries A.D.

In the meantime, from the days of the Roman republic to those of the Renaissance, India continued to suffer from and to absorb the effects of a series of invasions, and to be divided and redivided between a bewilderingly quarrelsome succession of separate states. For those invading India from abroad the valuable fertility of the Indus and Ganges basins was all too apparent. Moreover, India's trading links extended through the Arab world as far as the Roman Empire on the one hand and China on the other, and her rulers became bywords for wealth and their lands prized objects of foreign conquest. But the rewards for those leading an army out of India, through the Khyber or Bolan Pass to the mountains of Afghanistan or the deserts of northern Iran, were much less self-evident. The neighboring princedom within India was so much more accessible and the advantages of overrunning it so much more obvious. India at that time might well have been compared to a perpetual melting pot or cauldron to which fresh ingredients were periodically added but from which little was ever poured. So the brew grew stronger and more complex.

The Islamic invasions that preceded the Mughal Empire and the one leading to the empire itself were of a different kind, however. For the first time they brought with them an element that would not be Indianized and absorbed in the sense of being Hinduized. This element was Islam, of course, a religion as different from Hinduism in many respects as it was possible to be. And reciprocally, though there were conversions to Islam—mainly of those who had much to gain and, in the case of the lower castes, little to lose—India refused to be Islamized. At least three-quarters of the population remained Hindu. Yet under the Mughals well over half the country owed allegiance for the first time in centuries to a single ruler. It was therefore very much to the credit of Babar, the first Mughal emperor, and above all to that of his grandson, the great Akbar, that throughout the subcontinent Indians of the ruling and middle classes—Hindu and Muslim alike—felt a loyalty to the emperor, and through him to the state, of a kind that had not been in evidence for centuries.

In due course the old order changed, and among the Indian vultures squabbling over a disintegrating Mughal Empire there were European jackals—Portugal and Holland at first, followed by Britain and France—insisting on a share. The metaphor is too restricted, however, since the quarrel between Britain and France in India was a local manifestation of their worldwide rivalry, whether in Europe, on the high seas, or in North America. Ironically, moreover, the India that was later to become the jewel in Queen Victoria's imperial crown was initially seen by the British as very much a second-best trading venture. What they really wanted, and what the Dutch succeeded in denying them, was access to the islands of the East Indies, or present-day Indonesia—a much richer source of the spices that, in the days before refrigeration, were the Eastern treasure most sought after by Europeans. Thus it was that the British need to secure their trading rights in a part of the world plagued by political instability led to the only invasion in Indian history from the sea.

In 1751 Robert Clive, disgruntled clerk turned soldier in the employ of the British East India Company, won his first victory against the French and embarked on his meteoric military and administrative career. By 1818 the British had ensured their control of the whole of the subcontinent through direct rule or treaties with independent Indian states. In 1857–58 they survived the Indian Mutiny, in which Indian troops in regiments led by the British turned against their officers. This revolt may or may not have been sparked by the use of fat derived from cows and/or pigs to grease the cartridges of a new kind of rifle,[2] but it was definitely fueled by a British disregard for traditional values and beliefs in the course of "reforms" and "improvements" the British were imposing on a deeply conservative society. From that time until just after the turn of the century, with somewhat less disinterested high-mindedness and far-sighted wisdom than Kipling attributes to them, the British in India enjoyed their imperial heyday. Yet by 1947 both India and Pakistan had been given their independence. Empires, it seems, are not built to last now as they were in Roman times.

Much of the credit must go, of course, to Mahatma Gandhi. He was the first man in history to achieve such a large-scale victory against a well-armed opponent by entirely nonviolent means. Granted that when Brigadier General R. E. Dyer, brigade commander at Jullundur, ordered his troops to fire on the unarmed illegally assembled crowd of which Rushdie has Aadam Aziz be a member,[3] killing close to four hundred and wounding well over a thousand, he ensured Gandhi's ultimate triumph, though it took the British governing class another ten years to begin to realize this fact. Such inadvertent assistance in no way detracts, however, from the achievement of the man who so caught the imagination of the Indian in the street or the bazaar, who inspired such widespread and unflagging devotion over so many years, and who made so few concessions on matters of principle. It is thus strange that, with the exception of three things—the comment preceding Gen. Dyer's attack to the effect that "in Amritsar the Mahatma's grand design is being distorted" (35), Amina's relief that his assassin did not have a Muslim name, and Saleem's carelessly getting the date of Gandhi's death wrong—Rushdie ignores Gandhi in *Midnight's Children*. Or perhaps it is not so strange. The Mahatma's profoundly if unorthodoxly religious approach to politics, together with the way he almost singlehandedly ensured eventual Indian independence, led to Muslim alarm at the increasingly imminent prospect of a Hindu-dominated Indian government. An undoubted if unintended result of Gandhi's success was therefore to make the partition of India a precondition of its independence. And partition led in turn to the eventual establishment of an Islamic state in Pakistan, whereas Rushdie would clearly have preferred an undivided secular state of India.[4]

By the mid-1940s two world wars had greatly sapped Britain's ability and resolve to maintain control over a worldwide empire. And mercifully the surprise victory of the Labour party in the election of 1944, after the defeat of Germany, saved Britain and India from any danger of the kind of war France fought to postpone the inevitable in Indochina and Algeria. Nothing can alter the fact, however, that Gandhi greatly hastened the inevitable. And despite the tragic communal rioting at the time of independence and partition, during which between two and three hundred thousand were killed—Muslims by Hindus, Hindus by Muslims, and at least as many again by hunger and disease amid the chaos[5]—many more lives would eventually have been lost but for that haste.

In assessing the British role and British rule in India, one must acknowledge at the outset that they were undertaken to make a profit and maintained in order to continue to make a profit. It must also be admitted that the British created a denser-than-average smoke screen of hypocrisy to conceal any such motive from others and from themselves, and to many Indians their attitude must have been insufferably patronizing. Reforms were always chosen by the British and administered by the British, just as the need for them was used by the British as a source of continual reproach.

With that much conceded, it remains true that roads, railways, dams, irrigation systems, hospitals, schools, and colleges were constructed, that land was drained, that justice was administered with rectitude even if without much imaginative empathy, and that many Indians benefited from all of these achievements, even if some Europeans benefited more. Also, in contrast to what happened in many other colonies, enough Indians were given both the education and the experience necessary to have some chance of running a twentieth-century state successfully before being called on to do so, and despite the faults to which Rushdie calls attention, India is one of the few multiparty democracies still functioning in the third world. Finally, and most relevantly for the purposes of this study, Britain bequeathed to India a common language that all educated Indians learn and that does not give an automatic advantage (as does Hindi, the country's other official language) to those from a certain region. It is also a language that gives India easy access to the commerce, scholarship, news media, and literature of the outside world, and the outside world easy access to India—of whatever advantage or disadvantage that may be.

Religious Background

Hinduism   Those attempting to understand Hinduism from a Christian standpoint, however hazy, will find themselves, on the one hand, abandoning their preconceptions as to what a religion must include and, on the other, broadening their sense of what it may include. In the first place, Hinduism has no central source of authority, no inspired scriptures claiming to contain anything resembling a final answer, no creed or other means of testing orthodoxy, and no such concept as heresy.[6] What is true of other religions, though all too often either hotly denied or condemned—that is, that religious beliefs and practices change over the years as societies change, that they vary with the social background and level of sophistication of the worshipers, and that they need to change and vary thus—is an integral part of Hinduism. Indeed Hinduism is less a religion than a synthesis and less a synthesis than an anthology of all the practices and beliefs it has incorporated from all the religions it has absorbed.

The roots of Hindu belief lie in the four Vedas—ancient writings recording the philosophical and religious gropings of the early Aryan invaders, which are still revered but almost never read except by scholars. As Sarvepalli Radhakrishnan explains, "By progressing from the not unusual polytheism of the early Vedas, through monotheism, to suggestions of monism, these poems and songs [i.e., the mantras or first portion of each Veda] paved the way for the monistic tendencies of the Upanishads [i.e., the concluding portion of each Veda]."[7] Already, since it is possible to talk of polytheism, monotheism, and monism in connection with these very early holy writings, it is clear that Hinduism encompasses a wide range of religious and philosophical thought. The form the monism referred to above takes in subsequent Hindu thought is "the belief in an uncreated, eternal, infinite, transcendent, and all-embracing principle, which, 'comprising in itself being and non-being,' is the sole reality, the ultimate cause, and foundation, source, and goal of all existence. This ultimate reality is called Brahman. As the All, Brahman causes the universe and all beings to emanate from itself, transforms itself into the universe, or assumes its appearance. Brahman is in all things and is the Self (Atman) of all living beings."[8]

Clearly such a nonanthropomorphic, abstract kind of mythology does not meet the needs of most worshipers. The One that is the All remains an element of Hindu belief, particularly as the "goal of all existence" or the All that those who escape from the imprisoning cycle of reincarnation rejoin. But for purposes of worship Brahman is personified, in its inactive role (of that which encompasses all being and nonbeing) as the rather vague figure of Brahma and in its more active aspects as both Vishnu and Shiva. For most Indians, however, even Brahma remains a shadowy unreality alongside either Vishnu or Shiva. Vishnu is usually seen as a manifestation of the loving and caring aspect of the All, while Shiva embodies its destructive potential as well as, paradoxically, its regenerative power. Many Hindus think of either one or the other as the exclusive embodiment of the creative function of Brahman and therefore as he whom they worship as the one God. Yet this conception is not seen as in any way denying the reality of the other of this pair of gods, since he remains the other side to the total reality of God/Brahman/the All. Vishnu, moreover, has down the ages taken the forms of a series of avatars or incarnations, both animal and human, in each case to rescue mankind from some grave danger. The most famous of these,

Krishna, is often viewed and worshiped in his own right as a god, as are many other lesser manifestations of the All. Shiva, in turn, compensates for being the embodiment of the obvious destructive aspects of the All by also being the god of sexual regeneration, as well as performing acts of Vishnu-like preservation in a number of myths.[9] His multiple personality is likewise reflected in the triple identity of his wife as Parvati (the lover), Durga (the mother), and Kali (disease and death).[10]

Out of this apparent confusion several clear truths about Hinduism emerge. First, there is no attempt to deny, conceal, or simplify the variety and complexity of the world we live in. By manifesting itself many times over, the One that is the All preserves the unity of all things while also acknowledging their bewildering and contradictory diversity. For what the monism inherent in Hinduism has always avoided is reducing such multiplicity-in-unity and unity-in-multiplicity to a simplistically polarized, Manichaean duality of black and white, good and evil. Thus Shiva is god of both destruction and re-generation, and in praying to him to preserve you, you are appealing to the likely source of what threatens you. Ultimate reality must include, incorpo-rate, and acknowledge what humans perceive to be the evil as well as the good in life, rather than merely disowning it by putting the blame on some agency other than the ultimate one.

Second, as India has absorbed wave after wave of invaders, so Hinduism has incorporated ritual after ritual, deity after deity, and put them all to good use as manifestations of the variety and complexity of things. Thus Shiva is an amalgam of the Aryan god Rudra and the Tamil god Murugan, while his worship incorporates perhaps still older fertility cults centered on a phallic emblem or a bull, and his wife's manifold personality is clearly an amalgam of Aryan and pre-Aryan goddesses. Thus Ganesh the elephant-headed god was probably a totem god in origin, but he was (and still is) popular enough with the villagers for the priestly caste or Brahmans to make him the son of Shiva and Parvati and to invent a story to account for his head.[11] Thus, in a bold move to hasten the reabsorption of a Buddhism that, in India at least, was in decline, the ninth avatar of Krishna was de-clared to be none other than Buddha himself. Clearly Hinduism is a religion that functions more as a society than a religion in relation to myth, custom, and commonly held beliefs. Its dogmas change, adapt, and incorporate the new as necessary, without the need of papal or convocational approval. In-deed, as will become more apparent, Hinduism is very clearly social as well as religious in its nature and functions, as all religions once were.

Third, Hinduism allows for participation on many different levels in many different ways. There are thousands of strictly local gods and goddesses who remain unknown to anyone living more than a few score miles away but who are worshiped alongside Vishnu or Shiva or perhaps three or four of the major deities. Yet there are also devotees of Vishnu or Shiva whose dedication to the god of their choice is as monotheistic as that of Muslims to Allah or Christians to Christ. The Brahmans may use their influence to sway people's belief in this direction or that, just as teachers of English may fight a rearguard action on behalf of the possessive before a gerund or lead the attack on gender discrimination in language. But ultimately both are powerless to compel the tide of common usage or belief to change direction. From time to time, every religion must endorse or at least condone certain pieties and pietisms its intelligentsia would rather do without—*vox populi vox Dei*. But Brahmans do not personally have to believe in or practice a great deal of what constitutes Hinduism for villagers in Assam or Tamil Nadu—and vice versa. Hinduism has no monolithic administrative structure, no bureaucracy, and imposes no obligation to conform. To Hindus it seems not unreasonable that the One that is the All should manifest itself to, and be worshiped by, the diversity of humanity in a diversity of forms and ways.

A religion like this is likely to seem much less militantly certain of its own monopoly of truth, much less aggressively evangelical in its efforts to convert others, and much more tolerant of dissent both within and beyond its own ranks. True, Jainism and Buddhism are variants of Hinduism that have broken with the parent faith, but there is relatively little hostility between parent and offspring—except where, as in Sri Lanka, differences are intensified by linguistic and economic factors. Indeed, followers of any religion are regarded by Hindus as fellow seekers after truth, though curiously deluded in certain respects. Ultimately, of course, Hindus are just as sure as anyone else that they know best, though they are infinitely more patient with the obtuseness of others. What reason is there for them not to be, since they believe that almost all of us, Hindus included, will spend close to an eternity of trial and error before escaping this vale of tears?

Two further features of Hinduism make it unique among the world's major religions and must be mentioned since both have an enormous impact on Indian social norms and structures. The first of these is the belief in reincarnation, or transmigration of souls. More important than the process of being born over and over again, however, is the fact that one's status in the next life is determined not just by behavior in this life but by a karma or collective moral standing derived from all one's previous incarnations. If one thinks of the seeming impossibility of changing for the better in just one life, thanks to the deadweight of accumulated bad habits, wrong decisions, and failed resolutions, and then multiplies that by who knows how many thousand former lives, it is small wonder that karma has come to mean something very like "inescapable fate" in common usage. Like predestination in Calvinism, however, it is a comforting belief to the elect, or those whose caste implies the accumulation of such quantities of merit in previous existences as to defy rapid erosion. Unlike Calvinism or any form of Christianity, however, Hinduism has as its ultimate aim not the achievement of individual immortality, but the escape from the wheel of life—the treadmill of recurring individual existence—and the merging of oneself in the self-oblivion of the One that is the All.

One of the by-products, as it were, of the belief in reincarnation is the Hindu emphasis on reverence for life—a fellow feeling for all living things based on a sense of the unity of all life. The extremes to which this belief is carried in the case of the cow would seem to be a carryover from totem worship in some pre-Aryan source. At the other extreme, the care some Hindus take to avoid stepping on insects has never prevented other Hindus from making excellent soldiers.[12] Nevertheless, Gandhi's successful use of nonviolent tactics doubtless owed a lot to traditional Hindu values.

Reincarnation is not part of the Vedic worldview—what the Aryans brought with them to India. So it is presumably one of the elements that was incorporated into Hinduism from Dravidian or other earlier Indian sources. The caste system, however, is something the historian Romila Thapar records the Aryans as bringing with them in a rudimentary form. But the way in which they extended it after their arrival enshrines the Aryan response to their Indian experience. What had been a purely social or class division into three tiers—warriors or aristocracy, priests, and the common people—became a four-tier system with the lowest of these set apart by a combination of occupation, race, and color (*varna,* the Sanskrit word for "caste," literally means "color").[13] In modern times, the increasingly rigid hereditary basis for determining caste continues to emphasize the crucial importance of the last two factors. Moreover, as later "Aryan" conquerors from Britain were glad to borrow the caste system and solder their own "sahibhood" on to its upper end, so those earlier Aryans were perhaps glad to borrow reincarnation to explain, bolster, and justify their inherent pale-skinned superiority. Even today, moreover, Indian brides and bridegrooms with pale or "wheatish" complexions are considered to be the most desirable.[14]

Clearly, once castes became related to occupations, they tended to proliferate as the latter became more specialized. Thapar also argues that the caste system made it easier to fit new ethnic groups into the social system by allocating them a subcaste. Straightforward conversion to Hinduism is virtually impossible, however, since there is no real way to allocate traditional caste on the basis of an unascertainable karma. So, if new arrivals were to be fitted into the system at all, they had to be given their own special caste. It is hard to imagine a more inflexibly conservative social system, feudalism not excepted, or one more conducive to fatalism than a divinely ordained caste system. And it is just this fatalistic quality of Hinduism that Muslims, Jews, and Christians alike are likely to find hardest to accept.

Islam   Granted that everything, gods included, is a manifestation of Brahman or the One that is the All, it is still true that Hinduism has acquired more and more gods, and therefore has been able to express its sense of the nature of things in more and more diverse ways the longer it has been in existence. Islam, on the other hand, was founded above all else upon a rejection of the polytheism of pre-Islamic Arabia, and its convictions as to the nature of things flow almost exclusively from the assertion that there is one god only and his name is Allah.

Hinduism has no prophets, still less a single founding figure, and no single written source of authority. Islam owes its very existence to the Prophet Muhammad and finds answers for every kind of problem in the Qur'an, the inspired and definitive word of God as transmitted to his prophet via the Angel Gibreel (i.e., Gabriel). Moreover, though Islam recognizes such figures as Abraham, Noah, Moses, and Jesus as prophets before Muhammad, there is no purely Muslim tradition of slowly revealed, evolving truth such as is to be found in the Old Testament and such as has led to the wealth of subsequent Talmudic exegesis or to the New Testament and the similar establishment of Christian doctrine. Islam sprang fully grown and armed, like Pallas Athena, from the head of Muhammad. The authority of the Qur'an, moreover, is absolute to a degree that exceeds that of any other religious text. The most extreme doctrinal form this faith in the Qur'an takes is the assertion that its wording is "uncreated." That is to say, though it was first revealed through Gibreel to Muhammad, it has always been in existence as the word of God, much as Christian doctrine states that Christ, though "incarnated" during his earthly life, has always been in existence as a member of the Trinity.[15] Since the revelation of God's message is in as complete and reliable a form as the Qur'an, there has been no further need of prophets since Muhammad.

Hinduism has tended to spread by osmosis and absorption, Islam by the sword. Moreover, so successful militarily were the hitherto fractiously divided desert tribes to whom God's last word was initially directed that, within a century, Islamic armies had taken the faith as far west as Spain and as far east as India. And though it is true that conversion at swordpoint is not prescribed in the Qur'an, Islam and Christianity remain the two world religions to have recognized the concept of a holy war, which Muslims call a jihad.

More relevantly to the novels of Rushdie, Hinduism tends to be so ill-defined and inclusively adaptable as to be continually changing and yet never really change. Islam, by contrast, was dynamically flexible while Muhammad was still alive and new or revised revelations could be counted on to deal with new or changing circumstances, but it has become less so with the passage of time. An ironically relevant instance of the possibility of such flexibility in the early years can be seen in the incident of the satanic verses, which, though not recorded in the Qur'an, is attested to in oral and written sources of tradition.[16] These tell of an occasion when Muhammad received instructions from Allah via the Archangel Gibreel, authorizing him to reach an accommodation with the authorities in Mecca. The terms were to be that the three senior goddesses of the existing pantheon would be acknowledged by the new faith as retaining an intercessionary role not unlike that of the Virgin Mary in Catholicism. In return, all more minor deities' existences would be discontinued. Such instructions were subsequently countermanded by Gibreel and stigmatized as having originated during a satanic impersonation of his archangelic self. The possibility of skeptical or satiric use such as Rushdie has made of the incident has always existed, of course, so the tradition is one of those whose authenticity would seem to be guaranteed by the very fact that the episode is open to interpretations that are not to the credit of the participants. Alternatively, one Islamic scholar has argued that the incident of the satanic verses "was invented to illustrate the legal doctrine of 'abrogation,' according to which some Qur'anic verses are deemed to be superseded by others as sources of law."[17] Either way, the story illustrates or justifies lack of rigidity with reference to the Qur'an.

Such doctrinal flexibility was short-lived, however, predicated as it was on Muhammad's exclusive access to the divine mind.[18] After his death it became necessary to establish an authentic text of the Qur'an and an approved version of the many apocryphal sayings and legendary deeds of the Prophet, with the result that Islamic doctrine has tended to become more rigid over time.[19] And periodically such rigidity has helped lead to schism when changes have been felt to be necessary by some sizable minority.

Ironically, the only important surviving group that (itself subdivided) differentiates itself today from the Sunni (i.e., "traditional" or "orthodox") sector of Islam is the Shiah or Shiite sect, with its main strength in Iran. The split occurred in the first place over whether Muhammad's successor should be his son-in-law or the father of his favorite wife, but it ultimately led to the martyrdom of Husain, the Prophet's grandson. Largely as a consequence, Shiite belief acquired an almost Christian emphasis on suffering, and the schism persists as a doctrinal rather than an organizational dispute between an institutional orthodoxy and a more charismatic dissenting sect. Sunni Muslims seek a consensus whenever possible on any matter of controversy and accordingly tend to be very conservative. They were the ones who first declared the Qur'an to be "uncreated" and therefore immutable. The Shiites, in contrast, rely much more on the inspired leadership of their imams, of whom Khomeini was one, and have been wont to throw up new "messiahs," of which Khomeini was thought by many to be one, from time to time.[20] In the past therefore, the rigid fundamentalism that Rushdie attacks in *The Satanic Verses* has not tended to be found among Shiites.

Islam shares many of its characteristics with the other two great monotheisms to emerge from the deserts of the Middle East, which is scarcely surprising since Muhammad was clearly influenced by both of them, particularly Judaism. One might even go so far as to say that monotheisms as a species tend to display exclusivity and bigotry ("We alone have the truth!"), missionary militancy, and a proclivity (*pace* Jainism and Buddhism) to divide and subdivide into sects. More positively, however, Islam is clearly recognizable by Christians—especially Protestants—as a religion. Not only is there just one God together with a heaven and a hell complete with angels and devils, a set of scriptures, and a prohibition against drinking alcohol. There is also a clear acknowledgment of the equality of all men before God and in theory at least before their fellow men. (The status initially accorded women reflected the social structures of desert tribes as closely as those of Hindu, Jewish, and Christian women have tended to reflect equivalent social realities.) There are clearly delineated obligations to dependents, to servants and slaves, to the poor, and to society in general in the form of a moral code that served as a set of civil laws in the Islamic states of the new Muslim world.

The obvious decency of intent behind many such injunctions of the Qur'an, the black and white clarity and the unequivocal certainty of Islam's stand on many issues, even the harshness of its judgments and punishments, together with a nostalgic longing for the simpler world for which such laws were designed, combine to give fundamentalist Islam the same kind of attraction that fundamentalist Christianity has for many who are dismayed by the complexities and uncertainties of today's world. New converts to Islam, however, tend to be less selfishly preoccupied with individual salvation and immortality and more concerned with such issues as social justice. This behavior reflects the fact that, in the religion Muhammad founded, rendering to Caesar was indistinguishable from rendering to God, since church and state were one.

So far as Rushdie's novels are concerned, the chief interest and relevance of the religious background (apart from the specific issues that have led to accusations of blasphemy in the case of *The Satanic Verses,* which will be dealt with later) lie in the way both *Midnight's Children* and *Shame* display something of the ethos of the majority or official religion of the country in which each novel is wholly or predominantly set. It will be argued that, in style and tone rather than in specific content, *Midnight's Children* is a Hindu novel and *Shame* a Muslim one.

Political Background

It is usually assumed that politics begins more or less where history leaves off. Someone need only mention Northern Ireland, however, to remind us that history is still happening and that politics began centuries ago. Accordingly, as Indian independence approached and then finally arrived, old grudges were remembered and ancient animosities that had remained quiescent for decades erupted all over again. On the Hindu side there was a buried fear of and resentment toward those who had been their rulers for far longer than the British. And on the Muslim side there was fear of what that resentment would lead to under a government elected by the Hindu majority, together with a measure of disdain for their vegetarian, cow-loving, former inferiors. Under the British, however, it had been the turn of the Hindus to fare better than Muslims. Switching from one state of subjugation to another, they found it easier to accept British ways, attend British-run schools and colleges, and thereby secure government employment. This situation clearly led to Muslim resentment at having had to kowtow to Hindu babus (i.e., Indian clerks who could speak English) whom they held in contempt. Moreover, all such historical attitudes were exacerbated by economic factors in areas where, for instance, Hindu landlords and Muslim tenants or the reverse were the general rule.

Whether a united independent India could have survived is an unanswerable question. What is clear is that the British refused to recognize the inevitable until far too late, and continued (whether deliberately or from sheer force of habit) their traditional policy of "divide and rule" by encouraging the Muslims to think in terms of partition. As a consequence, far too little time was left for an accommodation to be reached between the Congress party and the Muslim League. What is equally clear, however, is that the two Indian parties played the roles in which Britain had cast them, the Congress party through insensitivity to Muslim fears and the Muslim League through sheer intransigence.

The main pressure for independence had come from the Congress party, which was predominantly Hindu but at least nominally secular and which claimed to represent all Indians. Muhammad Ali Jinnah himself, president of the Muslim League at the time of independence and the first governor general of the new nation of Pakistan, was for a number of years a member of both the Muslim League and the Congress party, at which time he was strongly opposed to political policies based on religion and was regarded as anti-Muslim by Muslim fundamentalists. But the phenomenal success of Gandhi's nonviolent campaign against the British, as well as his strong influence over the Congress party, gave the independence movement an increasingly Hindu character and drove Jinnah to take up a more partisan position.[21] Therefore the almost exclusively reactive preoccupation of the Muslim League was to fight for partition, whereas an integral part of the Congress party campaign was the drafting of plans and programs for a future government of an independent India.

The outcome was that, after partition and independence, Congress was able, as the ruling party in India, to carry out those policies it had been so busy preparing. The Muslim League, in contrast, had few plans ready to be put into effect in Pakistan. In addition, India was heir to the whole apparatus of government under the British—the capital city, the buildings, most of the civil service, the police and army headquarters, and so on—whereas Pakistan had to choose its new capital, create a bureaucracy and the administrative machinery needed by a modern state, and set about trying to hold together the two very diverse halves of Pakistan, separated by 900 miles of hostile territory, so as to turn them into a single nation.

India was lucky in its first prime minister, Jawaharlal Nehru. It may even have been lucky in the assassination, less than six months after independence, of Mahatma Gandhi, the father of that independence. Had Gandhi lived longer, he and Nehru would undoubtedly have clashed. Indeed, at the time of his death Gandhi had begun a fast aimed in part at the government's refusal to let Pakistan have its rightful share of unspent taxes collected before the British left India. But the tragedy left each man in undisputed possession of his own piece of history: Gandhi, the idealist fighting for a cause; and Nehru, the politician, able to do what was necessary to take and hold power—great power, both at home and on the world stage—yet never be seriously corrupted by that power.

Nehru was not able to accomplish all he wanted to; he was not able to

change as much as he felt needed to be changed about a deeply conservative, tradition-bound society. But he held together the extraordinary diversity of languages and cultures that constitutes India for as long as he lived.
Apart from two short periods when Lal Bahadur Shastri and Morarji Desai
held the prime ministership, either Nehru, his daughter (Indira Gandhi—
Rushdie's character the "Widow"), or grandson (Rajiv Gandhi) have until
very recently headed the Indian government. Yet despite the appearance of
a dynasty that this continuity of power presents, India has remained a parliamentary democracy with fairly regular elections and peaceful changes of
the party in power, as when Indira Gandhi was defeated in 1977 and when
she returned to power in 1980. That for no very clear or good reasons she
declared a state of emergency two years before her defeat—an emergency
that Rushdie incorporates in *Midnight's Children*—is a serious blot on
India's democratic record. That she called the election in which she was defeated is a tribute to that record.

By contrast, democracy in Pakistan has had a rough ride. For the first ten
years of the country's life, heads of state and governments changed almost
with the seasons.[22] Finally the army seized power in a coup d'état Rushdie
describes in *Midnight's Children* (279–82) and refers to in *Shame*.[23] The
first elections since independence (representatives elected under the British
in 1946 had governed up to that point) were then held under a highly pa-
ternalistic form of democracy designed by Field Marshall Ayub Khan and
known as "basic democracies." The field marshall was elected president and
exercised almost dictatorial powers until 1969; under him Pakistan took its
first steps toward becoming an Islamic republic.

Right up to 1971, however, Pakistani politics were bedeviled by the division between East and West Pakistan. The men of West Pakistan, living
in the area bordering Afghanistan and Iran through which most invasions
of India have taken place, tend to think of themselves as fighting men de-
scended from fighting men. Those of East Pakistan, now Bangladesh, are
physically smaller on average, have a much less turbulent history behind
them, and are more likely to show pride in their Bengali language and culture (which they share with Hindu Indian Bengalis) than their prowess
with arms. To generalize even further, with religious affinities and differences set aside, antipathies between West and East Pakistan resembled
those between Muslims and Hindus that precluded a united independent
India. In addition, the center of political power was always in West Pakistan, as were government industrialization projects and other attempts at
modernization. As the East Pakistanis were wont to complain, however,
most of the nation's foreign-exchange earnings came from the sale of jute

grown in East Pakistan. Small wonder East Pakistanis remembered that many of them had not been in favor of partition when it was first mooted and had given it their eventual support on the understanding that there would be two independent Muslim states. This bitter division within the nation was reflected in the election of 1970, when Zulfikar Ali Bhutto (Rushdie's Iskander Harappa) and his Pakistan People's party won a resounding victory in the western part of the country. Sheikh Mujib, however, won an even more resounding victory in the more populous eastern part and would have held a parliamentary majority. The West Pakistanis refused to tolerate such a situation, and their response precipitated the breakup of the country—an event that figures prominently in both *Midnight's Children* and *Shame* and that will be examined below as part of the joint story of Indo-Pakistani relations since independence.

To remain with exclusively Pakistani affairs for the moment, Ali Bhutto's second victory at the polls, in a Pakistan shorn of its eastern wing, figures even more prominently in *Shame*. Like Nixon's second successful bid for the presidency, it was an election Bhutto could have won easily without cheating, but he was determined that the victory should be so resounding that all memories of previous defeats (by Kennedy or by Mujib) should be silenced for ever. Thus the first prime minister of Pakistan to hold the post with any semblance of a democratic mandate, who could have remained in power using none but democratic means and helped establish a tradition of doing things democratically, in effect offered power straight back to the army.[24] Specifically Bhutto indulged in election irregularities that gave his enemies the opportunity to have the election overturned by General Zia Ul-Haq (Rushdie's Raza Hyder). And Zia, despite many promises, did not call an election to restore democracy for the next eleven years. In addition, of course, Bhutto opened the way for Zia to turn Pakistan into more of an Islamic state than ever—something Rushdie cannot have regarded with favor.

Perhaps the dominant feature of the history of both India and Pakistan since independence, however, has been the hostility between the two nations. Initially this centered on Kashmir, home of Rushdie's Aadam Aziz and largest of the independent Indian states under British protection, with a 77 percent Muslim population, a Hindu maharaja as ruler, and frontiers with both India and Pakistan as well as Afghanistan and China. The ruler, by the terms of the British offer of independence, was free to choose which of the new nation states Kashmir should join. He would have preferred Kashmir to remain independent, and his consequent prevarications are too complex to describe in detail. He made a provisional approach to the Pa-

kistanis, but they, suspecting this of being a cover for secret negotiations
with India, aided and abetted a raid in such force as almost to amount to
an invasion of Kashmir by Pakistani tribal bandits in search of loot. As a
prerequisite for help from Indian troops, Kashmir then formally acceded
to Indian rule. The case is still before the United Nations; India and Pakistan have a provisional frontier splitting Kashmir where the fighting finally stopped. All the choice areas fell to India, so Rushdie has Raza
Hyder become a national hero by capturing the Aansu-ki-Wadi, a valley
so high "your spit froze before it hit the ground" (82). Of course
Iskander—"Isky" of the golden thumb—buys the place for a song and
later turns it into a ski resort.

The most serious outbreak of hostilities between the two countries came
as a result of the dispute already referred to between East and West
Pakistan—a dispute arising out of the deadlock in the election results of
1970. Subsequent negotiations between Ali Bhutto and Sheikh Mujib having reached stalemate, Mujib was arrested and flown to the capital city of
Karachi, and troops from West Pakistan, where the majority of the Pakistan
army had always been recruited, in effect occupied East Pakistan. Widespread and indiscriminate raping and looting ensued—as part of the official
strategy, one presumes, for encouraging East Pakistanis to want to remain
part of a united Pakistan. (Rushdie records Saleem's inglorious role in these
events.)

Organized opposition was slow to develop, but mutinous Bengali elements
of the army began guerrilla resistance and were joined by young civilians.
Meanwhile, refugees—up to nine million, according to the World Bank—
streamed across the frontier with India,[25] giving that country a very material
as well as a political and humanitarian interest in finding some solution to the
problem. Weapons and training were offered to the guerrillas, and attempts
were made to persuade Europe and America to persuade Pakistan to make
political concessions that would persuade the refugees to return. Eventually,
after Pakistani planes attacked Indian airfields, the Indian army invaded East
Pakistan, capturing the capital city of Dacca within twelve days and making
prisoners of the entire Pakistani army in East Pakistan.

Subsequent events in the history of India include the electoral defeat of
Indira Gandhi, her return to power, and her assassination as part of the violence surrounding the attempt of the Sikhs in the Indian portion of the
Punjab to achieve self-government. In Pakistan there has been the impact
of the war in Afghanistan, the assassination of General Zia, the rise to
power of Ali Bhutto's daughter, Benazir Bhutto, as the country's first
woman prime minister in the first elections since those leading to her fa-

ther's downfall, and her own subsequent downfall. With the exception of the blowing up of an Air India jet by Sikh terrorists at the beginning of *The Satanic Verses,* however, none of these developments provides the raw material for Rushdie's fiction since the publication of *Shame.*

Chapter Three
Grimus

Gorfs live on the utterly barren planet of Thera, which "winds its way around the star Nus in the Yawy Klim galaxy of the Gorfic Nirveesu."[1] They look like enormous frogs, are made entirely of rock, and for many millennia whiled away their immobility in competitive anagrammatizing, or the tallest of ordering and reordering. Then one of their number (Gorf Koax) rethought their leader Dota's dictum, *"I think, therefore it is"* (79), so as to mean not so much that nothing exists unless conceived of as existing as that anything that can be conceived of as existing must consequently exist. He then proceeded to conceive of, or conceptualize, the possibility of another Dimension ("Endimions") in which some other form of life might exist, and from there he proceeded to create (or discover) a wide variety of alternative life forms throughout the universe. (The issue of creation or discovery is left moot, as is the question of whether Grimus and Virgil later find or create Calf Island: "Impossible to say whether we *found* the island or *made* it" [265].) And since there was now a motive for Gorfs to be mobile, Gorf Koax conceptualized a form of autotelekinesis "by a process of physical disintegration and reintegration" (247–48). Finally, since his fellow Gorfs were as alarmed as they were excited by these new developments, he conceptualized that for every conceivable Endimions there should be an Object by virtue of which, and *only* by virtue of which, communication and travel between that and all other Endimions (the spelling, singular or plural, is anagrammatically invariable) can take place.

Such Endimions can coexist temporally and spatially, interpenetrating and permeating the empty space of which each other's substance is chiefly made. By this means most of us, like the characters in the novel described in Jorge Borges's story "The Garden of Forking Paths," are leading many simultaneous and similar but continuously bifurcating and diverging lives in different Endimions. But many more Endimions are located over a widely scattered variety of planets. And it is on one of these that a young American Indian known as Flapping Eagle contrives, during the opening twenty-five pages of *Grimus,* Salman Rushdie's first published novel, to be orphaned and brought up by his sister Bird-Dog, to live for 777 years, and to end up on Calf Island. The longevity comes in a bottle—a yellow elixir that arrests the aging process and that Bird-Dog and Flapping Eagle are given by a peddler who turns out to be Grimus in disguise. Calf Island is the handiwork (or discovery?) of Grimus, who has stumbled on a Gorfic Object (a Stone Rose) and been enabled thereby to visit Thera and many other planetary Endimions, to bring back much knowledge and many artifacts (including bottles of immortality), and eventually to create what amounts to his own private Club Endimions somewhere in the Mediterranean—membership by invitation only from a variety of Dimensions; condition of membership, immortality.

Such are the basic premises of the fantasy cum allegory cum work of science fiction, *Grimus*. Its readers do not acquire all the above information immediately; some of it they must wait for until the closing pages. In the meantime, however, they learn that Nicholas Deggle, one of the three founding partners of Calf Island but subsequently exiled for attempting to break the Stone Rose, has used Flapping Eagle to test out an inter-Dimensional means of returning thither to carry out his revenge. And they eavesdrop on Virgil Jones, the other founding partner and first Calf Islander to greet Flapping Eagle, as he schemes to use the young Indian to overthrow Grimus's tyrannical rule. Utopia has somehow gone wrong, and its founder has conceptualized a mansion fortress within an impenetrable force field atop the island, where he lives with his Stone Rose and other Dimensional toys and his personal slave, Bird-Dog.

The rest of the island is being rendered progressively more uninhabitable by baleful emissions from the Stone Rose—emissions that are probably caused by the damage it sustained during Deggle's attempt to destroy it. The resulting attacks of what Grimus terms "Dimension fever" involve exposure to the "Inner Dimensions"—that is, awareness of the kind of reality or truth about itself that humankind cannot bear very much of. Virgil and his latest love, Dolores O'Toole, have escaped to the coastline, where the effects are as yet weaker. But most Calf Islanders manage to continue to live in K, a town high up on the mountain slopes and therefore much nearer and more subject to the Stone Rose, by maintaining such an obsessional preoccupation with day-to-day activities that they are able to deny the very existence of Grimus. In this denial they are led and inspired by Ignatius Q. Gribb, philosopher, high priest of the trivial, and student "of the most profound thoughts of the race, [as] tested by time . . . in old wives' tales, in tall stories, and most of all . . . in the cliché!" (160).

Flapping Eagle and Virgil climb the slopes toward K. The latter helps the former to cope with, and is impressed by his handling of, his first attack of "Dimension-fever," which is complicated by Gorf Koax, a meddlesomely curious onlooker. And the former is determined at long last to track down his sister and Grimus to obtain some antidote that will allow him to age in the usual manner. Approaching K, however, he is attracted by the idea of being able to settle down and lead a normal life among these other immortals rather than wander the earth like the Flying Dutchman. Unfortunately he is attracted by and attractive to Elfrida Gribb and Irina Cherkassova, the wives of K's two most prominent citizens. And when Elfrida tells her husband that it is Flapping Eagle she loves, the little philosopher dies within seconds from an overwhelming attack of Dimension fever.

Almost immediately the death of the architect of their chief line of defense against too much self-awareness is equally fatal to three other islanders. The remainder close ranks after the funeral, however, and Flapping Eagle and Elfrida find themselves ostracized and driven to seek refuge in the local brothel, which, as the indispensable dispenser of K's principal opiate, is accorded the status of a sanctuary. It is from here that Flapping Eagle launches his final attack on Grimus's stronghold.

Ironically, his chief ally in the assault is Grimus himself. For the master of Calf Island, able to monitor and control everything that happens on the island and much that does so elsewhere, is convinced that he has grown wise and powerful enough to have created "the Perfect Dimension" where everything is as he intends it to be. "To be wise and powerful is to be complete," he claims; then he adds, "*That which is complete is also dead.* And so I wish to die" (291). But his death also must be perfect, of course, and must include a successor to take over and maintain this private Dimension in existence. And the successor Grimus chose all those centuries ago, when Bird-Dog and her brother first became immortal, is his almost perfect double, Flapping Eagle.

In these circumstances, Grimus is clearly disinclined to give Flapping Eagle an elixir of mortality, and Flapping Eagle is more convinced than ever that the Stone Rose must be destroyed. Grimus, however, having irrevocably set in motion the mechanism leading to his own death, induces Flapping Eagle to join him in grasping the handles of a device called the Subsumer, which, he explains, will enable them to communicate with each other telepathically. What it in fact does is to mingle their personalities so that the Flapping Eagle in Grimus grows afraid of his approaching death, while the Grimus in Flapping Eagle tries to avert the destruction of the Stone Rose. In desperation Flapping Eagle grasps the Stone Rose and finds himself transported to Thera, where he consults Dota. And on his return he is able to compel the Grimus component of his joint personality to cooperate in deconceptualizing Calf Island and then almost immediately reconceptualizing it without the Stone Rose. But even Dota, leader of the Gorfs, had not been able to say whether an Endimions could continue to exist without its Object, and the book in fact ends with Calf Island "slowly unmaking itself, its molecules and atoms breaking, dissolving, quietly vanishing into primal, unmade energy" (319).[2]

Style

Those who first encounter *Grimus* after reading any or all of Rushdie's next three novels will, like a newly married couple exploring each other's family photograph albums, recognize the early stages of what they are familiar with in a later version. Those who read *Grimus* when it first came out, however, were probably as wide of the mark as to what Rushdie would make of his talent as most people are about what the children they know will make of their lives.

Stylistically there are suggestions of the post-Joycean liberties Rushdie later feels free to take with language, mainly in snatches or paragraphs (whether in first or third person) of interior monologue. Thus Dolores O'Toole, her relationship with Virgil Jones threatened by Flapping Eagle's arrival, tries to deny the latter's existence by insisting that there are only "Dolores O'Toole and Virgil Jones, Virgil O'Toole and Dolores Jones, Virgil Dolores and Jones O'Toole, Virgil O'Dolores and Dolores O'Virgil" (69). And thus Virgil, later, remembers the "snows of yesteryear." "Once. Then. Ago. Before. The terror of the titties, I. They came easily into my hands. They came. Easily. Gently does it, though some like it rough. Gently to the peaks of pleasure. Softly to the peaks of pain" (116).

Similarly, though the book as a whole is in the third person, there are portions of it not merely soliloquized but narrated in the first person or a mixture of first and third person: Flapping Eagle recalls his childhood, his exile from his homeland, his attack of Dimension fever, and—in I-Eagle and I-Grimus form—the mingling of his and Grimus's minds (15–23, 25–27, 84–85, 305–319); Countess Irina muses on Gribb's death (224–25). But there is little or none of the sheer linguistic exuberance to be found in Rushdie's next two novels. And there are only cautious flashes of the discontinuities and inconsistencies, whether temporal or narrational, that become progressively more outrageous in *Midnight's Children, Shame,* and *The Satanic Verses.* He has not yet found either the theme or the style that will allow him to be the writer he will in time become.

Science Fiction, Fantasy, and Satire

Grimus reveals an equal timidity, if one judges by later Rushdie standards, in its use of fantasy. To be sure, there is a dash of the mature Rushdie's insouciance when he not only has Flapping Eagle sail the same yacht for seven centuries but refers to an automobile on page twenty-five and a horse-drawn caravan ten pages and seven hundred years later, in each case as an apparently normal means of vehicular transport. Most of the book's unlikelihoods, however, are acknowledged as such by being given a quasiscientific explanation. Thus, by attributing extraterrestrial origins to the Elixir of Life, the Stone Rose, the Watercrystal, and the Subsumer, Rushdie implies that they function according to laws of physics that happen not to be understood as yet on earth. Even the concept of existence in a multiplicity of "Dimensions" could be seen as a fictional treatment of Hugh Everett's "many worlds" hypothesis to account for the paradoxes of indeterminacy in quantum physics.[3]

Rushdie disclaims any knowledge, at the time he was writing *Grimus,* of Everett's rather obscure and purely theoretical work.[4] In the later novels, however—and most remarkably in *Shame,* where the body's immune system becomes a symbol of crucial importance—Rushdie makes deliberate and far more important use of advances in scientific knowledge than in *Grimus.* Yet at the same time the fantastic, magical, and unbelievable elements to be found in *Midnight's Children* (principally the powers, both radiotelephonic and olfactory, of Saleem's nose, but also those displayed by other members of the Midnight's Children Conference, or M.C.C.), in *Shame* (the joint pregnancies of Chhunni, Munnee, and Bunny; Talvar Ulhaq's clairvoyance; the relentlessly arithmetic progression of the multiple pregnancies he imposes on Naveed; Babar's angelic transparency; Sufiya's blushing and final metamorphosis), and in *The Satanic Verses* (the twin protagonists' fall, unharmed, from 29,002 feet, and their subsequent angelic and satanic metamorphoses) are as pervasive as any equivalent in *Grimus.*

The crucial shift made by Rushdie between *Grimus* and *Midnight's Children* is that from science fiction to magic realism. However flippantly he wears his scientific mortar board in the former (his choice of stone frogs with a taste for anagrammatizing as the source of all life in the universe, for instance, invites a skeptical search for some meaning other than a literal one), the pretense is maintained that everything is explicable along conventionally rational lines. Whereas from *Midnight's Children* on, Rushdie's fictional world openly and matter-of-factly acknowledges the unmatter-of-fact to be a part of any vision of the world he shares with his readers. Perhaps the step is like that from the fiction of Jorge Borges to that of Gabriel Garcia Marquez. In the Borges's case a grotesque world of gigantic, all-encompassing lotteries, libraries, and labyrinths is buttressed and bolstered by so reasonable a tone of voice and so elaborate a scholarly apparatus of footnotes, referring as often as not to wholly fictional sources, that we are almost but never quite seduced into believing that the grotesque world we live in can also be reclaimed for sanity by a straight face and footnotes. Whereas in Garcia Marquez's work, no matter how hard the madness of magic struggles to keep pace, it still falls short of the insanity that realism has always managed to mask behind the straightest of straight faces.

So as a logical if seemingly paradoxical result, those books where realism is mingled with magic are the ones into which Rushdie has introduced such historical figures as Nehru, Indira Gandhi, Zulfikar Ali Bhutto, General Zia, Muhammad, and Margaret Thatcher. It is also in *Midnight's Children, Shame,* and *The Satanic Verses,* rather than in *Grimus,* that the author's social, political, and moral intentions are most in evidence. Rushdie, however, does not believe a creator of fictions can avoid making a political statement of some kind. Referring disparagingly, for instance, to a spate of movies and television programs about India that include *Jewel in the Crown, The Far Pavilions, Gandhi,* and *A Passage to India,* he argues that "the rise of Raj revisionism . . . is the artistic counterpart to the rise of conservative ideologies in modern Britain."[5] In the case of *Grimus,* though readers may not all be in agreement over just what it is that Rushdie intends to persuade them of, it is perfectly clear either that he set out with or that in the course of composition he developed some such intention.

A likely place to find social comment would seem to be the society set up by Grimus on Calf Island. But the messages it conveys seem contradictory. In the first place, the criteria by which individuals who must get along with one another for all eternity are chosen seem casual to the point of nonexistence. Admittedly, the suggestions Grimus puts forward may be meant as no more than an opening gambit: ". . . those with a pleasure in life. Those with a work to do which eternity would benefit. Those in short who would both benefit from, and seek, a longer span of life" (264). But the fact that this is the only explanation Rushdie feels a need to offer as to how the population of K was chosen offers little encouragement to those who hope to find sociological insight. Moreover, readers are surely not meant to be able to envisage what work such individuals as Count Cherkassova or Anthony St.

Clair Peyrefitte Hunter or Peckenpaw or Flann Napoleon O'Toole could claim to be engaged in that eternity would benefit.

Yet, tantalizingly, the social structure Rushdie announces as operating in K is communism in its final, ideal stage of "from each according to his abilities, to each according to his needs."[6] The farmers farm, the blacksmith hammers, the tavern keeper serves all who would drink, and the quartermaster distributes provisions from his store, each for no return other than being able to benefit from everyone else's labors. Rushdie is on record, moreover, as having Marxist sympathies, albeit less than perfectly orthodox ones.[7] But would he have his readers believe that, if only they possessed immortality and were no longer under any kind of pressure to achieve something new by the next decade, year, month, or week, they would be able to live in perfect harmony with one another? Surely not. With the notable exceptions of Norbert Page and the staff at the House of the Rising Son (the town brothel), there is very little evidence in *Grimus* of anyone serving or even seeming to be willing to serve anyone else. Rushdie's account of how the community works is purely theoretical—unrelated to the little that is actually shown of its workings.

An equally tantalizing prospect is offered, to those who know Rushdie's later work, by the thought of a whole community defending itself against self-knowledge through applying itself diligently to the pursuit of the trivial. The satiric potential of such a situation would seem to be limitless. But aside from a flick of the lash at Ignatius Quasimodo Gribb, Rushdie seems not to be interested in the faults of the men and women in the street in K. Their role is to be under pressure, from whatever it is that brings on Dimension fever and also from the burden of endlessness. Unlike the mythical Tithonus or Swift's Strudelbruggs, who must endure everlasting old age, most of these immortals are freeze-dried into an infinity of their thirties or forties. But the fact that they are frozen, that it is a living death they endure, is made clear by Flapping Eagle's desire to be able to resume aging and, most dramatically of all, by Irina's centuries-long pregnancy that can never reach term. With what irony, therefore, Ignatius Gribb begins his *All-Purpose Quotable Philosophy* with "perhaps the most perfectly all-purpose quote of all" (in acknowledgement of which Rushdie uses it as one of the four epigraphs preceding the novel): "The sands of time are steeped in new / Beginnings" (161).

Thus, Elfrida, Irina, Peckenpaw, Hunter, the Count, O'Toole, and all the rest are not prospective targets of Rushdie's satire, but victims of its true target—of Grimus. Grimus it is who has afflicted them all with the constant threat of Dimension fever and with an immortality that only Dolores and Liv are brave enough to end by slitting their throats. Grimus it is who must be destroyed.

But Grimus destroys himself. And Dimension fever is self-knowledge—not usually regarded as a reprehensible affliction. And the suicide rate, once some initial misfits had eliminated themselves, dropped to nil for many centuries until Flapping Eagle's arrival. And even Virgil's final cri de coeur, on the last page of his journal, refers to his marriage to Liv rather than to the state of the society on Calf Island and expresses an all but universal kind of disillusionment: "Beginnings are always better than endings. Then, everything was possible. Now, nothing is" (273).

In the main because his readers do not like most of the Calf Islanders enough to care what happens to them, Rushdie has a hard time making a convincing case for Grimus's demise. If he does succeed, it is on the grounds that humanity is not ready for the Stone Rose and all it brings with it. At this level the book becomes a rehash of a centuries-old debate on the dangers of too much knowledge—in particular, the dangers of too much scientific knowledge. As Virgil Jones explains to Flapping Eagle, the discovery "that we live in one of an infinity of Dimensions" (238) may entail so radical a redefinition of the nature of both humanity and the universe as to constitute an addition to human knowledge that should have been aborted. Later, when Flapping Eagle and Grimus have mingled their entities and their personalities, I-Eagle suddenly becomes aware of how, to his other I-Grimus self, "ideas, discoveries, learning" are all-important. So important, in fact, that they are to be preserved even at the cost of denying the remaining inhabitants of Calf Island the power to change the circumstances of their lives in the slightest degree, thus reducing them to "clutching obsessively at the shreds of their identity."

Not only is the reader unmoved, however, and indeed unconvinced by Rushdie's depiction of "centuries of wretched wandering" (317) on the part of his characters; the dilemmas of choice he presents are about as penetratingly and seminally original as the choice between exploring space and forgiving the third world its debt. The factors making for powerlessness, moreover, are much more likely to be social and economic than scientific. True, when Deggle accuses Grimus of playing God, the latter counters: "Would you rather . . . watch as governments used our gift to make weapons and war?" (264). And Flapping Eagle, watching Grimus disport himself childishly among his toys at the end of the book, muses: "Grimus: a baby with a bomb. Or a whole arsenal of bombs. On pedestals" (294). Both observations, in a book first published in 1975, might well have persuaded readers that the novel was about the atomic genie that should never have been let out of the bottle. But it remains difficult to identify the Dimensions, the Stone Rose, or a combination thereof, at all specifically with any actual or potential scientific discovery.

What emerges, instead, is a fashionably Luddite response to new scientific discoveries in general (to the release of nuclear energy at the time of writing, but equally applicable to genetic engineering or artificial intelligence) masquerading as a twentieth-century version of the Faust or Frankenstein myths. The story line is too complex, however, and there are too many loose ends and inconsistencies for the book to have the elemental power of such illustrious forerunners. Or is what Rushdie has in mind something much less specific? Are we to take Calf Island as the world as reconceptualized by Freud, Einstein, and Heisenberg (Grimus, Virgil, and Deggle?) and as now controlled by GM, IBM, and NBC (or Grimus, Inc.), with K as a world population hoodwinked into stupified acquiescence? Then again, there is always the "K" clue to a Kafkaesque reading, or the mountain as Jungian archetype. . . . And there is also the Persian poem in which thirty birds climb a mountain in search of a god called "Simurg" (of which Grimus is an anagram), only to have it dawn on them, on finding no one there, that Simurg consists of "si" and "murg" and means "thirty birds."[8]

Such a plethora of possible readings, none of which fits perfectly but all of which are interestingly if in some cases only marginally relevant, can be seen in retrospect to give promise or forewarning of the sense Rushdie claims to have tried to convey in *Midnight's Children* of a multitude of stories the reader merely touches on in following the thread of Saleem Sinai's autobiography.[9] In *Grimus* the effect this intention creates is lack of focus, rather than the richness of the later novels. But there do remain one or two further interpretations worth exploring.

Fawzia Afzal-Khan, for example, in a study that seeks to equate the post-Nazi situation of a writer like Gunter Grass with the postcolonial situations of Garcia Marquez and Rushdie, makes the ingenious suggestion that K "is, in fact, a 'colony' 'created' by the Gorfs, then 'ruled' for them by Grimus. . . . Thus, Grimus/Sispy becomes the prototype of the native-turned-colonizer, for he starts to rule Calf Island and its inhabitants in the way of the Gorfs."[10] The temptation to make such a parallel is obvious, despite the difficulty of seeing British or even French colonizers as impassive stone frogs of superlative intelligence. But the fact is that it was not the Gorfs—not even the renegade Gorf Koax—who created Calf Island. And the way Grimus "rules Calf Island and its inhabitants," so far from being "the way of the Gorfs"—whatever that may be—is something that, insofar as they are aware of it, they deplore. In the thought forms of Dota, "*It is a flagrant distortion of Conceptual Technology to use the Rose to Conceptualize a packet of* (he searched for the right form) *coffee*" (309). More will be said later on the subject of Rushdie and allegory; for the moment it is sufficient to say, perhaps regretfully, that Grimus is not a prototype of the Widow, Iskander Harappa, or Raza Hyder.

Probably the most interesting hypothesis as to the role Grimus plays in the novel, though only tenable in hindsight from a post-*Midnight's Children* standpoint, is that he is author of a text entitled *Calf Island*. Flapping Eagle can then be seen as a typical postmodern reader on a characteristic postmodernist quest—to kill the author. To dispatch himself, however, to say nothing of the author's author in the same fell swoop, might seem like overkill to even the most dedicated deconstructionist.

Within whatever kind of overall parable the novel constitutes there is a miniature one, told by Irina at the dinner table when Flapping Eagle meets the social elite of K, which may offer some guidance (175). The story recounts how the Angel of Death finds that, as he swallows each soul of a dead person, it becomes a part of him and he becomes less and less sure of his own identity and more and more depressed. So he asks God to relieve him of his duties. But God himself has grown tired of his job and wants to die. Clearly the Angel of Death cannot disobey a divine request that he swallow God. Doing so breaks his heart, however, especially when he realizes that he—that Death—cannot die since there is no one to swallow him.

Uma Parameswaran sees the real significance of the story (and indeed of *Grimus* as a whole) as lying in Elfrida's response to it.[11] "I don't like it," Elfrida says, predictably enough in view of the two women's already-burgeoning rivalry. Surprisingly, however, the neat, precise Elfrida goes on to say: "It's too pretty, too neat. I do not care for stories that are so, so tight. Stories should be like life, slightly frayed at the edges, full of loose ends and lives juxtaposed by accident rather than some grand design. Most of life has no meaning—so it must surely be a distortion of life to tell tales in which every single element is meaningful?" (175–76). Parameswaran is surely at least half right when she claims that "this statement epitomizes Rushdie's approach to the art of the novel," and it is certainly in accord with Rushdie's own comment, referred to earlier, about the effect he wished to create in *Midnight's Children* of a multitude of largely unrelated lives and stories going on within and around his narrator's life and story. Rereading *Grimus* after having read all three of his later novels, however, I see Rushdie as occupying a position closer to that of Flapping Eagle, who is almost equally attracted, for different reasons, to both of the women who are vying for his favors. Rushdie is in fact on record as feeling that "in India allegory is a kind of disease,"[12] and there is abundant evidence (particularly in *Midnight's Children* and *The Satanic Verses*) that Rushdie delights in "frayed edges," "loose ends," and "lives juxtaposed by accident rather than some grand [allegorical] design." Yet throughout all his work, cheek-by-jowl with, creating the need for, and counterbalancing this tendency to chaos, there is a constant fascination with pattern, with design, with linking chains of repeated images, motifs, names, and so forth. Compare, for instance, Dota's pronouncement, "*I think, therefore it is*" (66), Stone's "If it weren't for me the road would crumble" (105) as he counts the cobbles of K's main street yet again, and Grimus's "If I am to die without a successor the island will crumble" (298–99). Rushdie will return to the paradoxes of idealism with renewed vigor in *The Satanic Verses,* and the dichotomy between order and disorder, structure and energy reappears throughout his work.

Within *Grimus,* however, there is a more immediate and provocative subtext to be considered in connection with Irina's story. Reverting for a moment to the theme of a fear of new knowledge, Deggle, Virgil, and Flapping Eagle are not the only characters in the book to react negatively to radical innovation. Back on Thera (anagram of what may after all be the heart of the matter, and/or what it is advisable to keep our feet in contact with), the Gorfs honor their maverick innovator, Gorf Koax, with the title "Magister Anagrammari." They are nevertheless "not sure whether to cheer or throw brickbats" and must have their fears pacified by the provision of Objects to serve as the keys to inter-Dimensional doors (79–80). Later, moreover, their toadish leader, Dota, thinks—a bit too loudly, "like a man dealing with a stupid foreigner"—at Flapping Eagle: *"We have two great concerns. . . . The first is for the Gorf Koax, who has settled irrelevantly in your Endimions. Should you meet him, kindly let him know that his gross Bad Order has led to his being banned from Thera. He stands or falls with your Endimions"* (309). And fall he certainly does. The creator/discoverer of all other forms of life in the universe[13] (the origin of the Gorfs themselves being "lost in mystery")[14] meets his fate at the hands of one of his own creatures and is swallowed up, leaving no trace.

Overall, when compared to the later novels, *Grimus* lacks energy, stylistic assertiveness, and confidence in what it is attempting to be, but the potential for most such qualities is there. And in nothing is such potential more potently present than in this incipient Nietzschean black farce culminating in the death of God as a stone frog. It makes even *The Satanic Verses* seem innocuously tame. If that is Rushdie's intended message, it clearly self-destructs en route to the reader. But it is worth noting that his grasp, even in his notorious fourth novel, may have been exceeded by his reach in his first.

Chapter Four
Midnight's Children

I was born in the city of Bombay . . . once upon a time. No, that won't
do, there's no getting away from the date: I was born in Doctor
Narlikar's Nursing Home on August 15th, 1947. And the time? The
time matters, too. Well then: at night. No, it's important to be more . . .
On the stroke of midnight, as a matter of fact. Clock-hands joined palms
in respectful greeting as I came. Oh, spell it out, spell it out: at the precise
instant of India's arrival at independence, I tumbled forth into the world.
There were gasps. And, outside the window, fireworks and crowds. A few
seconds later, my father broke his big toe; but his accident was a mere tri-
fle when set beside what had befallen me in that benighted moment, because thanks to the occult tyrannies of those blandly saluting clocks I had
been mysteriously handcuffed to history, my destinies indissolubly
chained to those of my country.

Thus Salman Rushdie begins his second novel, *Midnight's Children*. In it
Rushdie returns to the India of his childhood; with it he wins fame, fortune,
and the Booker prize; through it he reaches readers all over the world, many
of whom will read his future novels but for a fair proportion of whom
Midnight's Children will remain their favorite and his masterpiece. From
those opening lines it is clear that the narration will be in the first person
and in a face-to-face, colloquial style, with the narrator at all times conscious of and frequently addressing his remarks directly to the reader. The
informality suggests a comic mode and the loose, rambling structure of a
somewhat picaresque bildungsroman. The reader also gathers that the
narrator-protagonist is just as old as the modern state of India, and might
assume that the author intends to make use of this carefully contrived
coincidence—even, perhaps, to have the recent history of the Indian subcontinent figure prominently in the story. But the most interesting clue as to
what to expect is to be found right at the outset. "I was born in the city of
Bombay . . . once upon a time. No, that won't do, there's no getting away
from the date. . . ." The first sentence begins factually before attempting to
escape into the language and spirit of fairy tale. The second one then drags
the reader back to reality, but fails—as do judges when cautioning juries to

ignore some juicy piece of hearsay evidence—to nullify the effect of that
"once upon a time." And there it is in a nutshell: the essence of magic
realism.

Saleem as Protagonist

These and many other features of the novel will need to be examined in
due course—most notably, perhaps, the fact that something like its first
quarter appears in most respects to be totally irrelevant to its remaining
three quarters. For the ancestry with which Rushdie provides his narrator-
protagonist, Saleem Sinai, and the family history that Saleem recounts with
such care are invalidated as soon as we learn how, from motives that have
nothing to do with the rest of the story, the nurse in attendance at his birth
switches babies. Once Saleem is in the bosom of his supposed and lovingly
unsuspecting family, of course, his relationships with them clearly help to
shape his future and that of the story. Yet the reader is by this time keenly
aware in the first place that things are not what they are assumed to be, and
in the second place that the narrator has known this since beginning the
story and has concealed the true state of affairs from the reader for as long as
possible. The implications of this second point I undertake, in true Rushdie
fashion, to consider later, along with many other aspects of *how* Saleem Sinai
tells us what he wishes us to know. For the moment, however, at the outset
of a brief survey of *what* he tells us, it is sufficient to note that he assumes
his role as both narrator and protagonist under something of a cloud.

Not that this is reflected in the narrative for some time. His father's assets, both financial and reproductory, may be frozen; his mother's verrucas
may play up; Mary Pereira may become Saleem's ayah out of a consuming
sense of guilt, thus attempting quite illogically to expiate her having
switched him from poverty to riches and his alter ego, Shiva, from riches
to poverty. But baby Saleem is the favorite of the hour. Even when he almost dies of typhoid, a kill-or-cure dose of snake venom saves him at the
last minute. And as the first baby to be born in an independent India, he
has his picture in the papers, he receives a letter of congratulation from
Prime Minister Nehru, and increasingly as the book proceeds he perceives
and wishes the reader to perceive the events making up his life as analogous to what is taking place in India as a whole. The reader knows, however, that all this is happening to the wrong baby—that Saleem's mother
died giving birth to him, that his true father is a poor street musician, and
that he is living in a lap of luxury he is not entitled to while the real Sinai
scion is being reared in the slums of Bombay. To look even farther ahead

than is Rushdie's wont, the ambivalence of the good-guy/bad-guy dichotomy enacted by Gibreel and Saladin (alias Gabriel and Satan) in *The Satanic Verses* is more than a little reminiscent of the double act put on by Saleem and Shiva in *Midnight's Children*. Indeed, Timothy Brennan would have us see the same doppelganger or "secret sharer" archetype in *Grimus* and his look-alike Flapping Eagle, and in the rivalry of Raza Hyder and Iskander Harappa in *Shame*.[1]

Fairly soon Saleem establishes that it is his role in life to be acted upon rather than to act. "From ayah to Widow," he himself admits, "I've been the sort of person *to whom things have been done*" (232, emphasis the author's). His sister is the one who acts and acts decisively, burning shoes when she wants attention and avenging herself ruthlessly on suitors (Sonny Ibrahim, Saleem) and rivals (Evie Burns) alike. Saleem, on the other hand, does things inadvertently. He starts a language riot because Evie Burns pushes the bicycle angrily away on which he is trying to impress her so that it runs downhill out of control into a protest march; he precipitates a passionate murder and a trial that goes all the way to the supreme court merely by trying to put a stop to his mother's innocent little meetings with her ex-husband. His most characteristic response to life is to find somewhere to withdraw from it all, whether a clock tower or the family laundry chest. And when he discovers how to use his telepathically sensitive sinuses, this ability enables him to become an eavesdropper extraordinaire. In this way he is the aural equivalent of Omar Khayyam Shakil, voyeur protagonist of *Shame*—the one a baby who never blinks (*M.C.*, 125), the other a child who scarcely sleeps (*Shame*, 15–16). Later he discovers that he is one of a group of preternaturally gifted children born in the first hour of India's independence. But even when greatness is "thrust upon" him and he discovers that his unusual powers enable him to act as telepathic receiver and transmitter by means of whom these children of midnight can communicate with each other in a nightly Midnight's Children Conference (M.C.C.)[2] held in Saleem's mind—even then his role is a largely passive one. Indeed, he goes so far as to regard the chaos and clamor of the M.C.C. as a refuge from his waking life.

The nearer to midnight the birth time of these extraordinary children, the more startling are their gifts. Saleem with his all-inclusive nose and power to bring together and Shiva with his invincible knees and power to destroy are the most strikingly endowed, with Parvati the witch and her genuine—as opposed to illusory—magical powers running a close third. When the novelty wears off and serious discussion over the future role of the M.C.C. leads to a showdown between Saleem's vague do-goodism and

Shiva's ruthless self-interest, there is of course no contest. Even without any help from Shiva, however, the M.C.C. contains the seeds of its own destruction.

Children, however magical, are not immune to their parents; and as the prejudices and world-views of adults began to take over their minds, I found children from Mahashtra loathing Gujaratis, and fair-skinned northerners reviling Dravidian "blackies"; there were religious rivalries; and class entered our councils. The rich children turned up their noses at being in such lowly company; Brahmins began to feel uneasy at permitting even their thoughts to touch the thoughts of untouchables; while, among the low-born, the pressures of poverty and Communism were becoming evident. (254–55)

The situation further deteriorates when an accident and a visit to a hospital reveal that Saleem's blood group is other than that of either parent and Mary Pereira subsequently confesses to what she has done. Obviously Saleem is much more uneasy thereafter about playing host to Shiva at meetings of the M.C.C. Once his family recover from their initial puzzlement and dismay, however, they discover that the revelation has not really made any difference. He is still his father's son; not even a thought is given to instituting a search for the real Sinai baby.

It is of some significance that, even before he has his sinuses drained and loses his powers of radiophonic telepathy, Saleem discovers they are inoperative as soon as the family crosses the Indo-Pakistani border. True, Saleem makes compensatory gains in status and self-esteem on his first visit to Pakistan, but only thanks to his cousin Zafar's enuresis. At a dinner hosted by Saleem's uncle, General Zulfikar, and attended by Commander in Chief Ayub Khan, the two boys are permitted to remain after the servants and women are dismissed. When Ayub Khan announces a coup d'état, however, Zafar cannot contain himself and is ejected in disgrace. So it is left to Saleem to redeem the family's honor by "capturing empty biriani-dishes with water-glasses" and "stationing salt-cellars, on guard, around water-jugs" (290) as his uncle outlines the plan of attack. After the coup, when the president is arrested and sent into exile, it is Saleem rather than Zafar who is awakened to accompany his uncle and watch a fat, middle-aged, naked man be marched to a waiting car with a gun between the cheeks of his "overfed rump" and to ride with him in that same car to the airport. This is to be involved in history more spectacularly than being born at the right midnight or disrupting a march with a runaway bicycle. But this is Pakistani history. Already, before writing *Shame,*

Rushdie has Saleem acknowledge in retrospect that "maybe this was the difference between my Indian childhood and Pakistani adolescence—that in the first I was beset by an infinity of alternative realities, while in the second I was adrift, disoriented, amid an equally infinite number of falsenesses, unrealities and lies" (326).

Pakistan is where Jamila, Saleem's sister, becomes a national sensation as a singer of uplifting, patriotic songs of such purity that she sings them through a hole in an embroidered sheet held up between her and her audience by two attendants. (So once her grandfather the doctor treated, wooed, and won her grandmother, whom he had only seen in successive seven-inch-diameter diagnostic glimpses though a hole in a sheet held by two burly female servants.) Pakistan is where, his sinuses drained and his nose no longer telepathic but supersensitive to odors it is exploring for the first time, Saleem encounters an ancient whore named Tai Bibi. She has such control over her glands that she can reproduce the spoor of anyone he describes to her. And it is she, hitting by accident on an aroma the irresistibility of which he has hitherto not let himself acknowledge, who discloses that his real love is his sister—something the latter, blood relation or not, is clearly horrified to learn. Pakistan is also where, returning home on his motor scooter during the Indo-Pakistani war of 1965, Saleem is concussed by a flying spittoon—a family heirloom propelled in his direction by one of the handful of bombs that kill all his relations except Jamila and an uncle in India—and is left with a memory wiped clean. And Pakistan is where, on the eve of West Pakistan's attempt to impose its will on East Pakistan, a Saleem who does not know that he is Saleem and does not know that he has a sister to pull the strings that put him where he is, finds himself in the army.

He is a private soldier but is employed as a tracker dog, so he and three young soldiers form one of several three-men-plus-a-dog teams sent to East Pakistan with the invading troops to sniff out "subversive elements." It is he who tracks down Sheikh Mujib, the East Pakistani leader, and, unremembering, watches him be arrested and flown off to captivity. But mainly this section of the book is remarkable for accounts of horrifying atrocities as seen through the initially amoral eyes of a Saleem whose mind is as cleansed of scruples as his sinuses are of mucus. Finally even he can take no more, and he leads his team away from the horror on a private nightmare pilgrimage through the swampily haunted jungles of the Ganges Delta's Sunderbans. Rushdie describes the journey as "among my favourite ten or twelve pages to write," and sees it as the "descent into hell" that any true comic epic should include.[3] There eventually Saleem is bitten by a snake whose venom, instead of killing him, restores his memory. There, in a strangely ecumenical episode, three Muslim boys and their aging man-dog spend many nights in a deserted temple dedicated to Kali, making love to "four young girls of a beauty which was beyond speech" who ominously remind one of the boys of the promised "four houris awaiting him in the camphor garden" should he be killed in battle (355). Thence all four emerge in some sense cleansed—though the three young soldiers are all too soon gruesomely dead. More scenes of horror are followed by the arrival of a victorious Indian army, only too happy to be invited to "liberate" East from West Pakistan in a campaign that has seen a certain Major Shiva become a national hero. Among the entertainers following the army is Parvati, who recognizes Saleem (M.C.C. transmissions having included telepathic images of each child viewing itself in a mirror), makes him her own personal prisoner of war, and causes him not only to vanish but to dematerialize in order to smuggle him back to India.

The final section of the book is so angrily written as to be more like a curtain up on *Shame* than a curtain down on *Midnight's Children.* For the first time in the novel we see Saleem passing political judgments that in many ways are naively reminiscent of his grandfather's bouts of optimism disease (39–40). He looks to Picture Singh, for instance, "the Most Charming Man [and snake-charmer] In The World," to emerge from the magicians' ghetto where Singh, Parvati, and now Saleem live and, "at the head of a great jooloos or procession of the dispossessed, perhaps playing his flute and wreathed in deadly snakes, . . . [lead them] towards the light" (411). But while in Parvati's magic basket Saleem "learned what it was like, will be like, to be dead." Then, as part of the rebirth, he "discovered anger" (382). So when finally the Widow (i.e., Indira Gandhi), using the emergency powers she granted herself in 1975, orders the sterilization of all remaining children of midnight save Shiva,[4] Saleem cranks his anger to a climax before letting it subside to the tone of resignation he uses elsewhere.

Throughout this third and last book of *Midnight's Children,* however, Rushdie's anger frees itself from the earlier restraints of amiable humor. Saleem's amnesia and his almost drugged state of amoral indifference give free play to authorial implication and irony. As a result, the horrors of the war in East Pakistan are exposed in a manner unmatched elsewhere in his fiction. In particular, his treatment of Indira Gandhi as the Widow "out-Swifts" Swift. Granted, he may deal with the shortcomings of Pakistani politicians at greater length in his next novel, *Shame.* He may present them as disposing of their political enemies in a ruthless and even gruesome manner.

But in the later book none fry their prisoners' testicles and then feed them to the dogs in the street. It seems he would have the Widow say, so much for all those liberated energies associated with independence and symbolized by midnight's children. Small wonder one of Indira Gandhi's sons did not hesitate, when the chance presented itself, to ban the sale of *The Satanic Verses* in India.

Also in this final book there is the strange relationship between Saleem and Parvati to be considered. Clearly attracted to his old M.C.C. ally against Shiva, Saleem nevertheless finds himself unable to make love to her from the very first time they share a bed. In her he sees, and in her he continues to see and will always see, a face that begins to change into that of his sister Jamila—into a vision of what, in his eyes, "had begun to rot, the dreadful pustules and cankers of forbidden love . . . spreading across her face" (383). Afflicted thus by emotional impotence, Saleem takes refuge in what is as yet a feigned physical impotence. So in despair, Parvati remembers his alter ego and uses her magic to entice Shiva into a passionate and stormy relationship that lasts until she becomes pregnant. Then by marrying her off to Saleem, Rushdie ensures that her child, elephant-eared Aadam Sinai and "true son of Shiva-and-Parvati, [as was] elephant-headed Ganesh," should be "true great-grandson of his great-grandfather" (405), Aadam Aziz. Thus Saleem Sinai, usurper of the place in the family history that should have been Shiva's, restores Shiva's son to his rightful name and role and, bowing out of the story he has chronicled, self-destructs.

The close of the book has struck many readers as pessimistic. As will be noted later, however, Rushdie himself has argued that there is enough variety and vitality throughout the book to act as a countervailing tendency. In a curious way, moreover, Saleem's castration and impending disintegration merely fulfill the sense throughout the book that his role is to be the onlooker, the voyeur, and that he is therefore by definition sterile. Whether by sitting atop a tower eavesdropping on all India, or by fighting a war with water glasses and pepper pots, or by falling incestuously in love with a sister who is not his sister (who is Shiva's sister!) and thereby incapacitating himself as anyone else's lover, or most crucially of all by having someone else's birthright thrust upon him, Saleem disqualifies himself for any role other than onlooker. Why else should Rushdie have provided him with over a hundred pages of spurious ancestry if not to hand it on to someone it belongs to? So, having disburdened himself of his role in the events he describes, for Saleem to remove himself from the scene leaves the stage clear for Aadam Sinai to resume the story—and India perhaps to resume the history—that should have taken place.

Size, Scope, and Multiplicity

No mere summary can hope to capture the range and variety of *Midnight's Children*. To take but one aspect of the novel, the assumption that social and political satire is restricted to its final book ignores many of the rapier thrusts with which Rushdie scores en passant. Not only do we in preindependence days, for instance, "look down on Breach Candy Swimming Club, where pink people could swim in a pool the shape of British India without fear of rubbing up against a black skin" (94); we also see how, after independence, when "India's first swimmer of the English Channel" attempts to gain entry to the same pool, "hired Pathans seize him, Indians save Europeans from an Indian mutiny as usual, and out he goes" (125). As already noted, Saleem discovers that Brahman children of midnight "feel uneasy at permitting even their thoughts to touch the thoughts of untouchables" (248); he then assumes, telepathically and successively, the identities of a rich landlord ordering the destruction of surplus grain, a starving child, a Congress party worker bribing a village schoolmaster to use his influence with voters, and Nehru adjusting the Five-Year Plan so as to harmonize with the predictions of astrologers (171–72). Still later he concludes that "in a country [i.e., Pakistan] where truth is what it is instructed to be, reality quite literally ceases to exist" (315). Yet one cannot say of *Midnight's Children*, as one can of *Shame*, that its predominant tone is satiric. The targets for such satire are too scattered, and there is too much else going on. The same is true of so many other characteristics to be found in the novel, moreover, that in the end perhaps the only general statement one can safely make is that the essence of *Midnight's Children* lies in its sheer size and scope and multiplicity. And among the more interesting of Rushdie's fictive strategies are the means he employs to hold things together as, for well over four hundred crammed pages, his novel deploys a named cast of more than seventy, occupies a stage stretching from Kashmir south to Bombay and from Karachi east to Dacca, and encompasses the history of India from independence to the state of emergency decreed by Indira Ghandi.

Rushdie himself has said of the novel: "One reason the book is so long is . . . the idea of the novel being something that includes as much as possible. It seems to me really that there are only two kinds of novel. There are novels which proceed on the basis of excluding most of the world, of plucking that one strand out of the universe and writing about that. Or there are novels in which you try to include everything, what Henry James called 'the loose, baggy monsters' of fiction."[5] Echoing Elfrida's opinion in *Grimus* that Irina's parable is too "tight" and that "[s]tories should be like life, slightly frayed at the edges" (*Grimus,* 175–76), Rushdie even claims that "one of the deliberate efforts in the book was to leave loose ends: I was very interested in the idea of implying a multitude of stories in one's structure, through which one picked one narrative path. There are stories you just happen to bump into and that you never see again, or stories that are just fragments of themselves and not completed. It was structured to contain that kind of material in it, because that was part of what I was trying to say."[6] Examples of such "material" are presumably to be found in the pages dealing with Commander Sabarmati's trial (*M.C.,* 252–57), Cyrus Dubash's reincarnation as Lord Kushro (260–62), Major Latif and his seven daughters, of whom Saleem has only to choose one and her natural teeth will be replaced with gold ones (302–304), and the white beggar Amina encounters on her way to have her child's fortune told—the one whose husband was killed in the independence riots (82).

Similarly, Rushdie has his narrator, Saleem Sinai, ask, in relation to an artist whose paintings start as miniatures but catch elephantiasis, "[I]s this an Indian disease, this urge to encapsulate the whole of reality?" (75). To this Richard Cronin, in a study of *Midnight's Children* and *Kim,* replies that "only those like Rushdie [and Kipling], who write about India in English" are likely to catch the disease and have the temerity to tackle India in its entirety.[7] Throughout what is a far more ambitiously ramshackle novel than *Kim,* however, Rushdie has created a web of things that, taken simultaneously, are intended to create coherence—repeated images, motifs, coincidences, and other stylistic devices such as were noted in *Grimus* but that are deployed here on a vastly more heroic scale.

Rushdie's prose style alone shows both the effort involved and the strains inherent in such a task. The penultimate paragraph of the book, for instance, from "I will have train tickets" to the end, foresees the remainder of Padma and Saleem's marriage day, recapitulates for the last time the preceding events of the story, and closes with the "fission of Saleem . . . bones splitting breaking . . . bag of bones falling down down down" as Shiva and the Widow close in on him from either side, all forty-five lines of print without a period (445). Earlier and similar passages capture "the confusion inside [Saleem's] head" when he first discovers his telepathic powers (168–69), the conflicting points of view expressed at a typical session of the Midnight Children's Conference (M.C.C.) in the "parliament of [Saleem's] brain" (222–23), and the tension-filled thirteen days of Parvati's labor and the Widow's refusal to resign (403–404). But much the most complex is the paragraph devoted to the bomb explosion that kills Saleem's family (332–33). A change from past to present tenses, the more striking for occurring midway through a single sentence, marks the crucial turning point—the onset of Saleem's amnesia. And no other passage in the book incorporates so much important ongoing action, so detailed a recital of past events, and such a wealth of implication for the future, all interwoven within a single syntactic unit. All such instances of recapitulation and/or foreshadowing, moreover, considered singly and collectively, are also among Rushdie's most frequently used and effective devices for creating unity out of a diversity that sometimes verges on chaos.[8]

And yet, unlike the extended sentences of Proust, James, or even Faulkner, Rushdie's retain their spoken quality by being largely typographical—breathless for lack of periods that the fastidious reader adds silently, but lacking in any sustained structural complexity. The example on pages 168–69 acknowledges as much by supplying uppercase initial letters without preceding periods to mark where new sentences might begin. Rushdie thereby achieves, stylistically, a coherence that he simultaneously acknowledges, stylistically, to be unachievable.

Two further purely syntactic or typographical expedients can be seen as performing similar functions. There is, in the first place, Rushdie's fondness for running words together, whether adjectivally, as in "Talldarkandhandsome" (101), or merely in commaless asyndeton, as in "their heads were full of all the usual things, fathers mothers money food land possessions fame power God" (223). More interestingly, there is his use of the colon to call attention to a grouping of items requiring emphasis. "What leaked into me from Aadam Aziz: a certain vulnerability to women, but also its cause, the hole at the centre of himself caused by his (which is also my) failure to believe or disbelieve in God. And something else as well—something which, at the age of eleven, I saw before anyone else noticed. My grandfather had begun to crack" (267).[9]

Thus all such syntactic efforts to hold things together also imply, by their very presence and nature, the centrifugal force of the diversity that makes them necessary, as do the equally frequent foreshadowings and recapitulations. And the same applies to imagery and events implying fragmentation and reassembly. Aadam Aziz must put together his bride-to-be from successive circular installments glimpsed through a hole seven inches in diameter. Amina sets about loving her entire husband by concentrating her affection separately and successively on "every single one of his component parts, physical as well as behavioural" (68). Ahmed dreams of reassembling "the Quran in accurately chronological order" (82). And Lifafa Das strives desperately to achieve universality by adding more and more disconnected pictures to his peep show (75).

More important than any of the factors hitherto considered, however, is Saleem Sinai himself. His role as a narrator will be considered later. Yet even without examining that aspect of his function, it is clear that his multiple personality and the frequently asserted metaphoric equivalence of his life story to that of India constitute the novel's most extraordinary bid for unity. He is, in the first place, the biological son of William Methwold and Vanita, the unwittingly adopted son of Ahmed and Amina, and the subsequently presumed son of Wee Willie Winkie and Vanita—that is, the joint product (as is India) of Hindu, Muslim, and English influences. In a quite literal sense, moreover, he is Shiva as Shiva is he. And subsequently he acquires, as further father figures, Nadir Khan the might-have-been father, Dr. Schaapsteker who brings him back from death, General Zulfikar who disowns his own son in Saleem's favour, and Picture Singh who adopts a reincarnated Saleem after his annihilation to invisibility by Parvati. As Saleem puts it, "my inheritance includes this gift, the gift of inventing new parents whenever necessary" (107–108).

Even more strikingly, once he discovers his unifying role vis-à-vis the 581 surviving members of the M.C.C., he becomes the living embodiment of this symbol of young hope—hope too soon to be crushed—in a young country. Only through Saleem's mind, the forum in which they are able to talk to one another, can the collectivity of the M.C.C. exist. When he first learns to use his telepathic powers he even believes "that I was somehow creating a world, that the thoughts I jumped inside were *mine,* that the bodies I occupied acted at my command" (172). On the very first page, moreover, he asserts: "I have been a swallower of lives; and to know me, just the one of me, you'll have to swallow the lot as well." Later, claiming that "I am everyone everything whose being-in-the-world affected was affected by mine" and, more humbly by this stage, that "each 'I', every one of the now-six-hundred-million-plus of us, contains a similar multitude," he repeats "for the last time: to understand me, you'll have to swallow a world" (370).

This insistence on Saleem's multiple personality is reminiscent of the capacity of the individual, as postulated in *Grimus,* to exist simultaneously in a multiplicity of different dimensions. In Saleem, Rushdie has created a unidimensional equivalent of such multidimensionality. Is it fanciful to go a step further and argue that Saleem is a simultaneous equivalent of reincarnation? Would this argument imply that *Midnight's Children* is in some implicit way a Hindu novel? Rushdie himself certainly sees a similarity between his kind of novel and the spire of a Hindu temple, "a representation of the world mountain" which "is crowded . . . [and] swarms with life, all forms of life. So the idea, the purpose of the temple is to include as much life as it can." Subsequently he identifies such inclusive pluralism with India rather than with Hinduism. "The . . . nature of Indian culture has always been multiplicity and plurality and mingling. Indians have always been good at taking from whoever comes in. . . . They assimilate the elements that are interesting and reject the rest. So Indian culture is not purist; the people . . . who talk most violently about purism in Indian culture tend to be Hindu religious extremists, and in Pakistan, similarly, the people who talk about a pure culture tend to be Muslim religious extremists."[10]

Such pluralism in Indian culture, however, is to a large extent the product of pluralism in Hinduism, whose multiplicity of deities and avatars bears witness to the number of other religions it has been able to incorporate and reincorporate, in contrast to the exclusive nature of Islam and other monotheisms. "It is this synthetic vision of Indian philosophy," argues Sarvepalli Radhakrishnan, "which has made possible the intellectual and religious tolerance which has become so pronounced in Indian thought and in the Indian mind throughout the ages. Recent squabbles between religious communities, bred of new political factionalism, are not outgrowths of the Indian mind but, instead, are antagonistic to its unique genius for adaptability and tolerance, which takes all groups and all communities into its one truth and one life."[11] So *Midnight's Children,* as a novel that tries "to include everything," is broadly synthetic and Hindu in spirit up to where Saleem loses his memory.

As already noted, the reassembling of fragments and the struggle to unify implies fragmentation and diversity. And further factors that contribute to the unity of *Midnight's Children* do so even more paradoxically than those already considered. Far more unifyingly pervasive than efforts at reassembly, for instance, is the drift toward disintegration throughout the novel. True, all of Rushdie's first three novels end in disintegration. The island that Grimus constructs literally deconstructs, "slowly unmaking itself, its molecules and atoms breaking, dissolving, quietly vanishing into primal, unmade energy" (319). And *Shame* ends in language—"the fireball of her burning," "the cloud, which rises and spreads and hangs over the nothingness of the scene" (286)—that is clearly meant to evoke a nuclear holocaust. But the disintegration of Saleem, with which *Midnight's Children* ends, is foreshadowed throughout the book. "Please believe that I am falling apart," he pleads as early as page 37—a fate he continues to remind us of until it finally takes place. Aadam Aziz's bones disintegrate until his legs give way; Amina disintegrates less specifically under the ministrations of Alia; Ahmed is discomfited by jinn, tetrapods, frozen financial and reproductive assets, postindependence pallor, and a stroke; and all three are dispatched by the same bomb. Parvati appears to begin to "rot," and Picture Singh collapses like a fallen tree. Also to be noted are the dismemberment of Hummingbird by assassins and of assassins by dogs, the malodorously decomposing antiquity of Tai the boatman and Tai Bibi the prostitute, and the self-inflicted leprosy of Musa.

What constitutes the chief agent of "deconstruction" in the novel, however, is its narrative mode and tone. Admittedly the very fact that everything is transmitted to us through a single narrator, omnipresent and obtrusive, makes for a kind of unity. Even the achronological and fragmentary nature of what he tells us lends a kind of authenticity to its disorderly inclusiveness. But such aspects of his role cannot gainsay the fact that Saleem is one of literature's most consummately unreliable narrators—a factor that would seem to add discontinuity rather than cohesion to the book. He openly acknowledges misdating Gandhi's death and the election of 1957. He admits, equivocally, "To tell the truth, I lied about Shiva's death" (427). And his analysis, Polonius-like in its absurdity, of the passive-metaphorical, passive-literal, active-metaphorical, and active-literal links between India's history and his family's (232–33) undercuts the reliability of his version of both. Those who painstakingly argue for a consistently analogical allegory of the Indian political scene[12] are surely misreading the disrespectfully deconstructive tone of the whole novel, to say nothing of Rushdie's comment that "in India allegory is a kind of disease," followed by an assertion that "the book clearly has allegorical elements, but they don't work in any kind of exact formal sense; you cannot translate the structure of the book into the secret meaning, the book is not a code."[13]

Most ostentatiously of all, of course, Saleem lies to us about his parentage, or refrains from telling us the truth, for close to a quarter of the book. That his disclaimer to Padma that "I provide clues" (118) won't wash is all too obvious from this panegyric to his grandfather's nose: "I wish to place on record my gratitude to this mighty organ—if not for it, who would ever have believed me to be truly my mother's son, my grandfather's grandson? . . . On Aadam Aziz, the nose assumed a patriarchal aspect. On my mother, it looked noble . . . the Brass Monkey escaped it completely; but on me—on me, it was something else again. But I mustn't reveal all my secrets at once."(15). As John Stephens shows, we have no idea who the Brass Monkey is as yet, no reason to think that "who would have believed . . . ?" is a real rather than a rhetorical question, no cause to see a literal rather than a purely idiomatic meaning in "something else again," and therefore no grounds to suspect that "all my secrets" implies more than a narrator's normal concern to create suspense.[14] Such hints can only operate retrospectively.

More serious, in Stephens's view, is the dual account of Saleem's amnesia. First we are told he is hit on the head by a flying spittoon. But later Saleem apologizes retrospectively for the apparent exploitation of a cinematic cliché in this episode: "With some embarrassment, I am forced to admit that amnesia is the kind of gimmick regularly used by our lurid film-makers. Bowing my head slightly, I accept that my life has taken on, yet again, the tone of a Bombay talkie; but after all, leaving on one side the vexed issue of reincarnation, there is only a finite number of methods of achieving rebirth"(339). "The relationship between these two accounts of Saleem's amnesia is a microcosm," insists Stephens, "of the operation of retrospectivity and deconstruction in *Midnight's Children*,"[15] and the same could presumably be said of the whole paragraph in which Saleem later asks, "[W]ould Mary's confession have come as a shock to a true telepath?" (443). Yet does allowing a first-person narrator to indulge in discussions of fictional strategy do more, in fact, than blur the distinction between him and his author in an interesting, perhaps revealing way? We should not forget that, in rewriting his mammoth first draft, Rushdie switched from third-to first-person narration.[16] And certainly, before reading a full-blown, self-consciously postmodernist, deconstructive intent into the second version of Saleem's amnesia, we should recall Rushdie's claim that the narrative technique used in *Midnight's Children* is owed in far greater measure to an Indian tradition of oral narration, complete with frequent metafictional comments on the course of events, than to "Garcia Marquez, Günter Grass," et al.[17] Should we suspect, moreover, that like Saleem he is withholding at least part of the truth, confirmatory evidence exists that Rushdie is not the first Indian author to employ metafiction.[18]

On the basis of such unreliabilities and inconsistencies, however, Stephens proceeds to call in question the final castration and to draw from the novel the implication that "history is meaningless" (206). Yet even if we accept that Saleem's castration is all in his mind—a mere extension of the "Saleem-equals-India metaphor"—does this imply that the Widow did not castrate India, or that Rushdie has no political point to make? Surely, moreover, to cavil over such details in a work of magic realism like *Midnight's Children* is to "strain at a gnat" of inconsistency and "swallow a camel" of magic. For the more willingly we suspend it, the more palpable remains our underlying disbelief. That so persuasively improbable a tale be told by so patently implausible a narrator is of a piece; the former virtually necessitates the latter. And so far from fragmenting the novel further, the combination adds to its unity—a unity of tone that incorporates the incredible and the inconsistent into the very texture of the writing.

Magic Realism

Magic: as in *One Hundred Years of Solitude* when Gabriel Garcia Marquez has Remedios the Beauty, in the act of helping to fold sheets in the garden, rise on a passing breeze and, accompanied by the sheets, disappear slowly into the upper atmosphere. *Realism:* as when, in the same book, workers on a banana plantation complain to the courts that the company pays them in scrip that they can only spend in the company store (on Virginia ham shipped in returning banana boats), that instead of installing permanent toilets it provides portable latrines, and that the company physician never prescribes anything other than a pill of copper sulphate, whether for "malaria, gonorrhea, or constipation." However, "the sleight-of-hand lawyers proved that the demands lacked all validity for the simple reason that the banana company did not have, never had had, and never would have any workers in its service because they were all hired on a temporary and occasional basis. So that the fable of the Virginia ham was nonsense, the same as that of the miraculous pills and the toilets, and by a decision of the court it was established and set down in solemn decree that the workers did not exist."[19]

Before one assumes absurdities that only magic realism can incorporate into its fictional world to be the prerogative of Latin America, it should be remembered that in 1928 the supreme court of Canada reached the unanimous decision that women did not enjoy the right of "all persons" meeting the stipulated requirements for senators to in fact become senators, on the grounds that a woman is not a "person." Nevertheless, as a literary mode magic realism may safely be assumed to be indigenous to South and Central America and to be in part the result of the region's multiple and blended cultures. Varying in number and proportion, the ingredients thereof are American Indian, Iberian (i.e., hybrid European Catholic and North African Muslim), West African, Indian, Chinese, and, most recently, European intellectual and North American capitalist in origin.[20] In addition, the introduction of nonrational, "magical" elements into an otherwise apparently realistic, rational world serves as a subversive rejection of the overwhelmingly scientific, rational approach to life of a culture that, in an ostensibly postcolonial world, still colonizes and still paternalizes, but economically and culturally more than militarily.

The aim of the magic realist is far from being always political and/or satirical, of course. The juxtaposition of fact and fantasy in his or her work may be as innocent of irony as that of science and superstition in the minds of New York commuters riding the subway and consulting the stars via the morning paper. The mere coexistence in time and space of so many different life-styles, cultures, and modes of perception is bound to lead to a climate of the miraculous. In the global village we are increasingly aware of inhabiting and for many writers besides those from Latin America, the stranger-than-fiction quality of so much truth requires a truth to more than realism on the part of fiction. But it is also clear that the stranger-than-fiction or dreamlike quality of much political life, and not merely in Latin America, is best satirized by being shown to be more incredible than the wildest fantasy. So when Saleem sets forth his narrative techniques as consisting of "matter of fact descriptions of the outré and bizarre, and their reverse, namely heightened, stylized versions of the everyday" (214),[21] he is at least acknowledging their potential for just such satiric effect.

At first sight India would seem to be almost as fertile a ground for magic realism as Mexico or Brazil. Its many languages, its variety of religions together with the enormous variations of practice and belief within Hinduism, and its hierarchy of castes are like geological strata marking the inundations of successive invasions from the north. Then, as a final overlay, there is the influence of two centuries of British rule on India's form of government, legal and educational systems, and the like. The officers' messes of the Indian army, for instance, have preserved the authentic atmosphere of the Kipling era far more faithfully than their British counterparts. And probably most important of all, there is the influence of English as the nation's only true lingua franca. All this would seem to make for as rich a potpourri of cultures as that of Latin America.

There are differences, of course. India, though often fragmented, has known itself to be a distinct entity—defined and delimited by the Himalayas and the sea and possessed of and by an ancient and unifying Hindu culture—since long before the Spaniards and Portuguese gave Latin America its superimposed linguistic and religious unity. Thus the paradoxes and incongruities of India have in most cases been part of the texture of Hinduism for far longer than those of Latin America have been incorporated into that of Catholicism. However, the British acquired India some time after Spain and Portugal appropriated the southern half of the New World, and they merely governed and exploited their possession, rather than settling and exploiting it as was the case in South America. So they never came near to imposing a unifying language on the subcontinent, as they did for instance on North America. As a result, the loyalties of Indians today are un-easily divided between the old languages, in which lie their cultural roots, and the new language, which is the only one by means of which all educated Indians can be reached as well as the one in which the world's business, education, science, and technology is increasingly conducted.

To the extent, therefore, that Rushdie is Indian and that his Indianness includes elements of Hinduism, his use of magic realism to accommodate the incongruities of his fictional world may have a distinctively Hindu and correspondingly inclusive quality to it. To the extent, however, that by going to school and university in England and writing his novels in English he has gained the whole world but lost his Indian soul, his use of magic realism and other self-conscious devices of contemporary fiction is likely to be less the spontaneous outgrowth of his Indian roots than the product of European and South American influences and to be correspondingly satiric in intent.

He himself is quite insistent that his narrative techniques have been strongly influenced by those of professional storytellers in India—though whether, as he would sometimes have us believe, this influence has been greater than that of the Western authors most commonly seen as his literary models is altogether another matter.[22] Elsewhere he has also written:

There are books that open doors for their readers, doors in the head, doors whose existence they had not previously suspected. And then there are readers who dream of becoming writers. For these . . . there are . . . books which give them permission to travel, so to speak, permission to become the sort of writers they have it in themselves to be. A passport is a kind of book. And my passports, the works that gave me the permits I needed, were *The Film Sense* by Serge Isenstein, the "Crow" poems of Ted Hughes, Borges's *Fictions,* Sterne's *Tristram Shandy,* Ionesco's play *Rhinoceros*—and, that summer of 1967, *The Tin Drum.*[23]

As for the role played by magic realism in *Midnight's Children,* Rushdie's first extensive use of the device shows clearly that he is not greatly interested in exploiting its satiric potential. But then, as already argued, *Midnight's Children* as a whole is much less satiric than *Shame.* And the magic-realist elements of the novel become less and less important as the events recounted require a more and more sardonic tone. Magic proper, indeed, is almost entirely restricted to the talents and activities of the M.C.C. in general and of Saleem in particular. Other matters may be subject to comic or savage exaggeration or coincidence, as in Amina's phenomenal run of luck with the horses or the death of all Saleem's relatives but two on the night of 22 September 1965. Some incidents—such as the summoning of dogs to avenge his death by Hummingbird's final "hum," the freezing of Ahmed Sinai's testicles, and Saleem's inherent or acquired immunity to snake venom—are on the borderline of magic. Although of minor significance in themselves, through sheer accumulation they help acclimatize the reader to an ambient air of fantasy. Yet other elements—such as the culinarily coercive prowess of the Reverend Mother, Amina, Mary Pereira, and Saleem—combine to provide the book with a powerful controlling metaphor to be examined later. Generally, however, magic equals the M.C.C. and the M.C.C. equals magic. So it is imperative to consider more closely the role and significance of the children of midnight in *Midnight's Children*.

The first thing to note is that, of the original 1,001 or surviving 581, only Saleem, Shiva, and Parvati play a role in the book other than to take part in M.C.C. conferences in Saleem's head and to be victims of the Widow's purge. It is also emphasized that "not all the children's gifts were desirable, or even desired by the children themselves" (194). Most importantly, however, such gifts as readers are informed of—the gift "of stepping into mirrors and reemerging through any reflective surface in the land"; "powers of transformation" into wolves, dwarfs, giants; the ability to change sex at will; the ability to divine water, heal through laying of hands, wound literally with words, or blind literally with beauty; the inability to forget anything seen or heard; and so on (195–96)—are essentially the endowments of characters in folktale and legend. They may be meant to capture the surge of optimism that the birth of a new nation ought to occasion. They also are intended presumably to exemplify the kind of raw, anarchic creativity that Indira Gandhi felt a need to suppress. But in entrusting such a potentially significant symbolic function to embodiments of such stereotypical third-world superstitions, Rushdie is already laying himself open to a charge made much more vehemently since the publication of *The Satanic Verses:* that of "orientalizing" his fellow countrymen. This term means the perpetuation and strengthening of the conceptual stereotype according to which the Orient—by its mysteriousness, inscrutability, untrustworthiness, irrationality, sinister sexuality, and overall primitiveness—reassures the Occident as to its sensible, straightforward, reasonable, trustworthy honesty and its essential superiority, while at the same time retaining the exploitable fascination of the unknown and the forbidden.[24]

Clearly it is only because of the sheer abundance and variety of their special abilities, and not by virtue of any recognizably useful traits bestowed on them by the author, that members of the M.C.C. can be thought of as in any way embodying a hope for the nation's future. It may well be that

Rushdie has no wish to fall into the trap of proposing specific and refutable remedies for seemingly insoluble social and political situations. And it is perhaps as a response to the apparently overwhelming insolubility of India's problems that Rushdie's invocation of the energies and the magic of folktale and legend can most plausibly be justified. Faced with a comparably skeptical complaint that the "happily ever after" magic of fairy tales is escapist and therefore unsuitable for children, Bruno Bettelheim counters that, in order to cope with deep and unarticulated anxieties such as Oedipal and sibling rivalries or the fear of being abandoned, children need the depth and honesty of folktales that acknowledge the existence of such problems, and indeed of evil itself, and that offer the reassurance that magic is available and on their side. There even seems to be a strong echo of the way Bettleheim justifies the magic of fairy tales in Mary Pereira's "Anything you want to be, you kin be,/ You kin be just what-all you want" (*M.C.* 126, 370). For, as he goes on to point out, no amount of thinking or even knowing that one can do something, in the manner of *The Little Engine That Could,* will enable children of the wrong age to catch a ball, tie shoelaces, or glue paper houses together. Indeed, thinking one can do what one all too obviously cannot do can be profoundly discouraging. But the simple magic of growing up will make all such things possible.[25] And societies, nations, even the species as a whole have similarly achieved, in time, what no rational forecast would have deemed possible. So, answering complaints about "the way in which the central character ends in despair," Rushdie himself says: "I tried quite deliberately to make the form of the book a kind of opposite to what the narrative was saying. What I mean is that the optimism in the book seems to me to lie in its 'multitudinous' structure. It's designed to show a country or a society with an almost endless capacity for generating stories, events, new ideas, and constantly renewing, rebuilding itself. In the middle of that you have one rather tragic life. The two have to be seen together."[26] It would be naive to maintain that the failure of the M.C.C., from internal as well as external causes, counts for nothing. But considered overall, the powers suggested by the magic it embodies are a way of giving fictional expression to that "almost endless capacity."

Finally, the two children of midnight "born on the stroke of midnight" are given gifts that are intrinsically significant. "Saleem and Shiva, Shiva and Saleem, nose and knees and knees and nose . . . to Shiva, the hour had given the gifts of war (of Rama, who could draw the undrawable bow; of Arjuna and Bhima; the ancient prowess of Kurus and Pandavas united, unstoppably, in him!) . . . and to me, the greatest talent of all—the ability to look into the hearts and minds of men" (196).

This is only one of many references in the book to Hindu mythology,[27] Saleem himself bidding us "[n]ote that, despite my Muslim background, I'm enough of a Bombayite to be well up in Hindu stories" (149). It is also fair to say that Rushdie's whole handling of Shiva, Saleem's "shadow" or doppelganger, is quite Hindu in spirit. Nowhere is he held to blame, as the Widow is, for the destruction he brings about or makes possible. Perhaps, as with his divine namesake, he is the embodiment of a seemingly cruel, destructive, but inescapable aspect of the cosmos. Perhaps he is a "there but for the grace of God go I" acknowledgement of the reverse side to Saleem's—and everyone's—coin. Either way, he plays his part, even fathering Aadam Sinai, the embodiment of Rushdie's hope for the future. As for Saleem's gift, Rushdie would seem to be staking out a claim on his narrator's behalf—in almost a throwback to Joyce's Stephen Dedalus or Lawrence's Paul Morrell, but with postmodernist adaptations—to the status of artist as protagonist.

Saleem as Narrator

In describing how he went about writing *Midnight's Children*—and more importantly how he rewrote it, cutting it down to a 500-page "*Reader's Digest* condensed version" from a first draft that was twice that length—Rushdie acknowledges his debt to Saleem for taking over the narration. The first draft, written in the third person, "was a mess," he admits, and

I was wondering what to do about this, and I was also worrying about the Tristram Shandy problem, about the fact that Saleem . . . was not born until 150 pages into the book. . . . I thought that maybe what I would do was allow him to narrate the section before he was born so that at least his voice would be present. . . . [But] the moment he began to talk, it became clear that he was never going to stop. It was like a coup: he just simply took a deep breath and started talking, and 500 pages later he stopped . . . On the whole I was very grateful to him for taking over, because he was clearly able to do what I wasn't. So that was one, probably the major discovery in the book.[28]

In the absence of a manuscript of the first draft, one can only speculate as to what it was like. All Rushdie tells us is that when he began to write it "there was a very very large amount of material," that as in the final version the protagonist was not born until well into the story, that "the book was completely rewritten" and trimmed to less than half the size in the course of being revised, and that the process of writing the first-person second draft seemed to be taken over by Rushdie's chosen narrator—that is, it went much more smoothly.

One may safely assume that little was added and a good deal removed in the way of material during the revision and that the most important changes, since "every sentence in the first draft went out of the window, and new sentences came in through the door," were stylistic. Not that I am suggesting the third-person first draft showed no change from or advance over *Grimus* in its prose style. Clearly the narrative material of *Midnight's Children* demanded and must have received different handling even in its initial form. Equally clearly, as is demonstrated by *Shame,* a novel resembling *Midnight's Children* as it exists now could have been written in the third person, though there would have been some differences of tone. But the use of Saleem as narrator must have permitted, sanctioned, provided the excuse for, encouraged, and even necessitated the stylistic liberties that Rushdie found himself only too happy to take. As Diogenes Teufelsdrockh claimed linguistic freedoms that even Carlyle had hesitated to permit himself, so Saleem blazed a stylistic trail for Rushdie to follow.

Attention has already been drawn to Rushdie's gigantic sentences at such crucial junctures as the jumble in Saleem's head when he first discovers his telepathic powers, the onset of his amnesia, Parvati's prolonged labor, and the closing sequence of impending disintegration. Other much shorter passages that call attention to themselves include the recapitulation in which Saleem recovers his memory after a cobra bite in the Sundarbans (353–54) and the enigmatic foreshadowing of a riddling rhyming prophecy outlining the unborn Saleem's future life: "there will be knees and a nose, a nose and knees. . . . Washing will hide him—voices will guide him. . . . Spittoons will brain him—doctors will drain him. . . . Soldiers will try him—tyrants will fry him" (87). It almost becomes a stylistic mannerism that a recapitulation or a foreshadowing (of which there are many) is the occasion for one of Rushdie's parodic versions of a purple passage. What follows, for instance, is the dreamlike description of Saleem's nightmare about the Widow—prophetically ominous, did the reader but know it and as Saleem knows only too well.

No colours except green and black the walls are green the sky is black (there is no roof) the stars are green the Widow is green but her hair is black as black. The Widow sits on a high high chair the chair is green the seat is black the Widow's hair has a centre-parting it is green on the left and on the right black. High as the sky the chair is green the seat is black the Widow's arm is long as death its skin is green the finger nails are long and sharp and black. Between the walls the children green the walls are green the Widow's arm comes snaking down the snake is green the children scream the finger nails are black. . . . (204)

The curiously dated, almost Gertrude Stein quality to such a passage, however, leaves the reader in some doubt as to whether Rushdie intends his parody to be deconstructive or emulative in its effect. Ultimately, it is not the set pieces that give the book its quality or that the reader is likely to remember nearly as much as the day-to-day, page-by-page capacity of the prose to surprise, amuse, and delight. Farfetched enough for Donne and extended enough for Milton, there is the metaphor for Saleem (or Shiva) as an embryo: "What had been . . . no bigger than a full stop had expanded into a comma, a word, a sentence, a paragraph, a chapter; now it was bursting into more complex developments, becoming, one might say, a book— perhaps an encyclopedia—even a whole language" (100). There are coinings like "what-happened-nextism" (39) to meet the requirements of even a comic Hopkins. There is the breathless, layered way in which, when uncle Hanif takes Saleem to watch wrestling, the reader is inside the boy's head who in turn is inside Hanif's head, and all three are also watching the wrestling and listening to the mixture of English and Indian vocabulary as if they had always done so.

. . . we're sitting in excellent seats as floodlights dance on the backs of the interlocked wrestlers and I am caught in the unbreakable grip of my uncle's grief, the grief of his failing film career, flop after flop, he'll probably never get a film again But I mustn't let the sadness leak out of my eyes He's butting into my thoughts, hey phaelwan, hey little wrestler, what's dragging your face down, it looks longer than a bad movie, you want channa? pakoras? what? And me shaking my head, No, nothing, Hanif mamu, so that he relaxes, turns away, starts yelling *Ohe* come on Dara, that's the ticket, give him hell, Dara *yara!* (168)[29]

In contrast, there is the clear, comic economy with which Rushdie parodies the whole notion of history enacted in miniature in Saleem's life by having a coup d'état played out on his Aunt Emerald's dining table.

How we made the revolution: General Zulfikar described troop movements; I moved pepperpots symbolically while he spoke. In the clutches of the active-metaphorical mode of connection, I shifted salt-cellars and bowls of chutney: This mustard-jar is Company A occupying Head Post Office; there are two pepperpots surrounding a serving-spoon, which means Company B has seized the airport. With the fate of the nation in my hands, I shifted condiments and cutlery, capturing empty biriani-dishes with water-glasses, stationing salt-cellars, on guard, around water-jugs. (281)

Also apparently owed to the first-person nature of the narrative are the liberties Saleem takes with the proper sequence of events. It comes as a surprise, therefore, to learn that the third-person version of the story also had Saleem waiting for about a hundred and fifty pages before being born. We do not know, of course, whether on its very first page that earlier narrative established the birth as having taken place at the same instant India became independent. On the one hand, it would seem likely that so crucial a coincidence of new beginnings would come at the outset of any telling of the story. On the other hand, however, Rushdie tells us that "originally the first line of the book, which is now buried somewhere, was 'Most of what matters in your life takes place in your absence,'"[30] which suggests a beginning well before Saleem puts in an appearance. Whether or not the long loop backward in time in which the published version establishes Saleem's spurious ancestry was an out-of-sequence flashback in the original, however, it is the first and by far the most extensive of only three instances in the published novel where an event makes its only or most important narrative appearance out of sequence. The other two are the scene in which Saleem uses a certain sheet with a hole in it as a ghost's costume (32) and the death of Aadam Aziz (268–70).

What there are innumerable instances of, however, and what are much more metafictionally manipulative on Saleem's part than mere departures from sequence, are recapitulations of what has happened and foreshadowings of what has yet to happen. The latter Saleem refers to as "movietrailers" (336) in one of his frequent cinematic metaphors—a metaphor Nancy E. Batty has ingeniously expanded: "Saleem's employment of trailers, as we shall see, is pervasive, and it is complemented by yet another cinematic narrative device which Saleem does not consciously identify. A close examination of *Midnight's Children* reveals that the chapter by chapter progression of the novel resembles the structure of an episodic film, or serial, in which synopses of previous events provide a rhythmic counterpoint to the tantalizing teasers which anticipate events to come."[31] A major use Rushdie makes of these two devices of anticipation and recapitulation is to stitch together a narrative that might otherwise fall apart. What they also achieve, as Batty points out, is in the former case to arouse expectation, in the latter to slow the pace of narration, and in both, therefore, to increase suspense. But by far the most important function these elements of the narrator's self-reflexive commentary perform is to help meet the author's need, throughout the book, to examine the nature of fiction. They achieve this end in large part by entering into the relationship between Saleem and Padma, his long-suffering if often impatient audience and would-be wife. Indeed, her frequent but fruitless attempts to make Saleem's "other pencil work" (39), and his equally frequent hints as to the reason for its inactivity, constitute in and of themselves a major component of both the relationship and the premonitory foreshadowing. But there are many other ways also in which, among the new narrational features resulting from Rushdie's revision of his first draft, Padma is of major importance, second only to the first-person voice of Saleem.

Padma—her name both appropriately and ironically means "lotus," a flower known to villagers as "The One Who Possesses Dung" (25)—is an earthily sturdy stirrer of chutney at Mary Pereira's Braganza pickle factory where Saleem has taken over supervision, Mary having retired to look after young Aadam Sinai. Padma it is whose relationship with Saleem, together with her insistence that if he must write his life story he read it to her, provides his narrative with its frame. It is Padma for whom in spite of himself he is writing. And it is Padma who acts as both audience and critic, expressing her irritation with Saleem's narrative methods and with what she sees as his aesthetic as well as his physical impotence. "At this rate . . . you'll be two hundred years old before you manage to tell about your birth," she complains in an impatient outburst of "what-happened-nextism" (39). Admittedly, by thus voicing the criticism of at least some readers, she to some extent disarms it since, charmed though they may be by her "Grandma Moses" kind of directness, those with any pretensions to sophistication must dissociate themselves from such naive honesty. But there is much more to Padma than a mere foil to enable Saleem to shine the more brightly.

Timothy Brennan makes a case for Rushdie's having introduced her into the story to redress the social and political imbalance of the work by having her act as a counterweight to Saleem's all too obviously middle-class point of view.[32] Insofar as *Midnight's Children* concerns itself with the critique of postcolonial society in India that Brennan seeks to find in it, the observation is just. But even on an apolitical plane her woman-in-the-street, feet-on-the-ground common sense is important. It reminds us, despite its inconsistencies and limitations, of a kind of basic stability, worth, and even wisdom that intellectuals can all too easily lose touch with. The opening of book 3, for instance—the scene in which Padma weeps for the Sinai family, almost all of whom have been eliminated in the preceding chapter with such surgical brusqueness as to preclude any show of feeling in a reader sufficiently in tune with the Saleem-Rushdie narrative tone to have persevered thus far—is a good example of Rushdie's richly ambiguous handling of her role. For as well as prompting condescending smiles, the passage elicits our uneasy awareness of Saleem's failure, from start to finish of the book, to feel anything for anyone other than himself as strongly and as spontaneously as this. It would be out of key with the book for him to do so. But it is not out of key with the book that Padma should, nor that Saleem's rebuke that she should "mourn for the living" and "grieve for Saleem" (335) should win him scant reader sympathy. Uma Parameswaran characterizes her as "the collective unconscious, the spirit of the country. . . . the archetypal Earth-Mother put through the Rushdie anti-romance wringer,"[33] and even if this somewhat overrates her status, it suggests the double role in which Rushdie casts her. On the one hand Padma prompts a more sustained metafictional commentary on what he is doing by the narrator, while on the other hand she supplies a commonsense corrective lest Saleem and Rushdie take their postmodernist proclivities too seriously.

She also contributes to a pervasive ambivalence about artists and the artistic process. I have referred above to the unreliability of Saleem as narrator,[34] arguing that it is consistent with the magic-realist mode and contributes to a unity of tone within the book. But this same unreliability does nonetheless foster a skeptical attitude in the reader toward the narrator, toward the author, and toward language itself. As Keith Wilson has pointed out, moreover, there is an above-average number of failed, quasi-, or would-be artists in the novel.[35] They include Nadir Khan the poet, his painter friend whose pictures grow and grow, Lifafa Das and his expanding peep show, Hanif the film director, Picture Singh the snake charmer, Jamila the singer, and most importantly, of course, Saleem the writer. For he too, like the others, illustrates the unattainability of either universality or the kind of perfection that Hanif aims at in playing rummy—in a word, the essential fallibility of the artist and of whatever medium he or she uses. This failure is probably most apparent when Saleem first discovers his telepathic powers, feels he is "creating a world," falls into "the illusion of the artist," and thinks that "the multitudinous realities of the land," raw and unshaped, are the product of his gift (172).

By the time we first meet him, however, chastened and ready to record, painstakingly, the story of his life, he has also joined the company of the book's humbler but more successful artists. He has mastered the more quotidian, Padma-like skills of cooking and chutney making, raised to the level of an art by so many other characters in the novel that we are surely meant to see in a more positive light his ambition to capture the thirty years of his

life in thirty chapters and in thirty different flavors, each in its own jar. It is
in terms of the "pickling process" that he enunciates his aesthetic credo.

To pickle is to give immortality, after all: fish, vegetables, fruit hang embalmed in
spice-and-vinegar; a certain alteration, a slight intensification of taste, is a small
matter, surely? The art is to change the flavour in degree, but not in kind; and
above all (in my thirty jars and a jar) to give it shape and form—that is to say,
meaning. (I have mentioned my fear of absurdity.)
   One day, perhaps, the world may taste the pickles of history. They may be too
strong for some palates, their smell may be overpowering, tears may rise to eyes; I
hope nevertheless that it will be possible to say of them that they possess the authentic taste of truth . . . that they are, despite everything, acts of love. (444, author's ellipsis)

He has expressed this fear of absurdity much earlier, on the very first page
of the novel. "I must work fast, faster than Scheherazade, if I am to end up
meaning—yes meaning—something. I admit it: above all things, I fear
absurdity." The objection may be raised of course that, even if Saleem
thinks he is being honest, Rushdie may be using his protagonist's self-
deception ironically. But there are no ambiguities concerning those other
practitioners of the culinary arts, whether Mary Pereira, who stirred her
guilt into her chutneys so that those who ate them became "subject to
nameless uncertainties and dreams," or Naseem, whose "curries and meat-
balls of intransigence . . . salans of stubbornness and . . . birianis of deter-
mination" had a "counteractive effect" and "filled Amina with a kind of
rage" (138), or Alia, who destroyed Ahmed and Amina by means of that
which she had "raised to the level of an art-form: the impregnation of food
with emotions." Moreover, though Saleem insists that Alia "remained second in her achievements in this field [to] my old aya, Mary Pereira," he is
even more insistent that "today, both old cooks have been outdone [by]
Saleem Sinai, pickler in chief at the Braganza pickle works" (320). So we
need be in no doubt as to either Saleem's intent or his ability to carry it out
when his own green chutney rescues him from yet another visit to the
hospital—yet another attempt to save him from the madness of his
storytelling (205–206). Clearly Rushdie sees such art, when hard-won
and aware of its limitations, as hearteningly or terrifyingly meaningful,
and not at all absurd in relation to life—as possessing, at its best, "the authentic taste of truth" and issuing in "acts of love."
   It seems that the controlling metaphor of *Midnight's Children,* the
equivalent of self-rejection by the immune system in *Shame,* is the making

of chutney. Only through the lengthy, painstaking "pickling process" can the bewildering variety of ingredients that demand inclusion in the thirty jars be preserved. Only through the use of repeated stylistic devices, recurring images, and unifying themes can the impossibility of including everything, and the impossibility of knowing what is the real truth about anything (an impossibility Saleem's narration constantly underlines), be overcome sufficiently for the novel to have "shape and form—that is to say, meaning."

And *Midnight's Children* does have meaning—meaning other than a solipsistic preoccupation with the nature of its own fictionality. To reduce the story to being about Saleem and the family that discovers that it is not, yet still is, his, and that love is thicker than blood, or even about the tolerant, inclusive, and ultimately impotent (i.e., Hindu) Indianness of the M.C.C., as opposed to the intolerant war of partition in Pakistan and the equally intolerant Indian emergency decreed by the Widow, is to oversimplify things to the point of caricature. Nevertheless, this is a third-world novel, and readers from India and Pakistan are in much less doubt than those from Europe and North America that, like *Shame,* it has a satirically didactic meaning. But meaning deriving from shape and form has to be much more than what can be reduced to moral or political platitudes. And meaning in the case of *Midnight's Children* includes, though it does not consist exclusively of, the nature and function of the act of narration.

Rushdie, it seems, must subject his art to the prolonged interrogation entailed in having Saleem as his first-person narrator, and in acknowledging thereby all the pitfalls of human fallibility that such a role is heir to, in order to discover that it is nevertheless possible to create a meaningful work of literature. Only then can he be sure that, despite the unreliability of language, words can still communicate. Only then can the first-person narrator he found so invaluable when revising the manuscript of his third-person first draft be dispensed with. (It is Saleem's disintegration rather than his castration that we may discredit, except as symbolizing his no longer being needed and as supplying a sense of closure.) Only then is Rushdie able to mount as directly satiric and as political an attack as he does in *Shame.*

For many, however, reading *Midnight's Children* will still prove a richer if or because more confusing experience than reading *Shame*—an experience during which readers witness and participate in the creation of unity and meaning that incorporates and uses, without ever denying, such confusion. To say that language and meaning crumble, disintegrate, de-

construct themselves, only endlessly and phoenixlike to reconstruct themselves, is merely to say that they partake of and reflect the human condition, and they do so the more convincingly when they openly
acknowledge—indeed, when they exploit—such limitations.

Chapter Five
Shame

Style and Tone

Only a page or two into the novel, as old Mr Shakil lies on his deathbed and looks out over "the remote border town of Q." (3) from his bedroom window, he sees the symbolically cracked golden dome of the Hotel Flashman, hears "the music of the imperialists issuing from the golden hotel, heavy with the gaiety of despair," and curses it "in a loud, clear voice" (4). Perhaps in ironic memory of his years at Rugby School, Rushdie has named the hotel after Harry Flashman, the bad boy of Thomas Hughes's *Tom Brown's Schooldays*. Flashman in Hughes's story boasts no connection with India, however, so it is presumably Flashman as reimmortalized by George MacDonald Fraser that Rushdie has in mind.[1] And the Flashman of these later novels, though every inch the bounder and scoundrel that the Hughes version of his younger self shows promise of becoming, is a comic antihero. Perhaps the hotel acquired its name during Rushdie's revision of the novel's first draft, since the shift in tone from Hughes to Fraser is a prophetic parody of that between Rushdie's first and second drafts. The former he has described as "much darker, oppressively and unremittingly gloomy." He adds, however, that "although the relationship between Raza and Iskander is basically tragic, the actual figures are clowns—gangsters, hoodlums—and not people who deserve Shakespearean tragedy. So you have to bring comedy into it—you have to write black comedy, because they are black comedy figures—and I rewrote the entire book, making it lighter."[2]

Although *Shame* as published may be lighter than its first version, it has always been and still is darker than *Midnight's Children*. This observation in no way gainsays the many characteristics that the two novels share. Both deal with the political history of India and Pakistan; both are written in the magic-realist mode; both have narrators who do not hesitate to comment on the story they tell; both treat temporal sequence cavalierly and include extensive metafictional foreshadowing; and both employ a flexibly informal, not to say colloquial, prose style that on occasion runs to unusually long sentences.

Yet even in this last respect there are distinct and ominous differences between the two books. The two longest sentences in *Shame,* for instance, are
much more bitterly satiric as well as more tightly structured than any in
Midnight's Children, the second and longer one being a veritable pièce de
résistance. I refer, of course, to the description of Rani Harappa's eighteen
embroidered shawls (210–14), collectively entitled "The Shamelessness of
Iskander the Great." External "scaffolding" is provided by the shawls' being
introduced individually as "the torture shawl," "the swearing shawl," "the allegorical shawl," and so on. Within this overall unity, phrases and clauses
create structures of discrete parallelism, rise to periodic climaxes, and cohere
in identifiable subunits the length of normal sentences and paragraphs.
Consider, for instance, the following brief extract:

. . . and the election shawls, one for the day of suffrage that began his reign, one for
the day of his downfall, shawls swarming with figures, each one a breathtakingly
lifelike portrait of a member of the Front, figures breaking seals, stuffing ballot-
boxes, smashing heads, figures swaggering into polling booths to watch the peas-
ants vote, stick-waving, rifle-toting figures, fire-raisers, mobs, and on the shawl of
the second election there were three times as many figures as on the first, but despite the crowded field of her art not a single face was anonymous, every tiny being
had a name, it was an act of accusation on the grandest conceivable scale, *and of
course he'd have won anyway, daughter, no question, a respectable victory, but he
wanted more, only annihilation was good enough for his opponents, he wanted them
squashed like cockroaches under his boot.* . . . (193, author's emphasis)

Note the cohesion achieved by ". . . shawls, one for the day of . . . one for
the day of . . . shawls . . . figures . . . figures . . . figures . . . figures," and
the variety achieved by "figures breaking seals, stuffing ballot-boxes,
smashing heads," as opposed to "stick-waving, rifle-toting figures," these
two similar yet dissimilar grammatical units being kept apart by one of
roughly equal length in which "figures" is qualified by a single participial
phrase.

Finally, a kind of dramatic structure for the whole gigantic sentence is
supplied by the interpolated and italicized asides to Rani's daughter. They
also serve to remind the reader that this is a prose translation, if you will, of
the language in which Rani writes her shawls. And these expressions of her
silently accumulated anger she has spent many careful years composing. It is
only fitting, therefore, that Rushdie's prose style should reflect that care.
The two qualities of coherence and anger, moreover, characterize the novel's
other long sentence, in which Rushdie lists the absurdities he would be

obliged to satirize if his subject were the real Pakistan rather than his "fairy-tale" one (71–72). And coherence and anger are what, in large measure, distinguish this novel from its predecessor.

But to return to the beginning in preindependence unpartitioned India, Omar Khayyam Shakil, bastard son by an Englishman of one of the three Shakil daughters, Chhunni, Munnee, and Bunny (the other two sharing the joys and opprobrium of motherhood by undergoing simultaneous phantom pregnancies), is born in his grandfather's deathbed. This inauspicious start to life is followed by twelve years of imprisonment in Nishapur, "the high, fortress-like, gigantic residence" (4) that neither his mothers nor their servants ever leave after his birth.

Little (except freedom) was denied him. A spoiled and vulpine brat; when he howled, his mothers caressed him . . . and after the nightmares began and he started giving up sleep, he plunged deeper and deeper into the seemingly bottomless depths of that decaying realm. Believe me when I tell you that he stumbled down corridors so long untrodden that his sandled feet sank into the dust right up to his ankles; that he discovered ruined staircases made impassable by longago earthquakes which had caused them to heave up into tooth-sharp mountains and also to fall away to reveal dark abysses of fear . . . in the silence of the night and the first sounds of dawn he explored beyond history into what seemed the positively ar-cheological antiquity of "Nishapur," discovering in almirahs the wood of whose doors disintegrated beneath his tentative fingers the impossible forms of painted neolithic pottery in the Kotdiji style; or in kitchen quarters whose existence was no longer even suspected he would gaze ignorantly upon bronze implements of utterly fabulous age. (26, author's ellipses)

That Omar Khayyam should spend twelve years "inside that reclusive mansion, that third world that was neither material nor spiritual, but a sort of concentrated decrepitude made up of the decomposing remnants of those two more familiar types of cosmos. . . . a sweltering entropical zone in which, despite all the rotting down of the past, nothing new seemed capable of growth" (25), prefigures not only the shamelessly voyeuristic, amoral life he subsequently leads but the whole atmosphere of the novel. As Sura Prasad Rath argues, "The labyrinthine entrapment of Nishapur is not only a physical condition of life in the gothic mansion, it is also a spiritual malaise corrupting and consuming Pakistan and even the West."[3] It is certainly very apparent to readers coming to *Shame* from *Midnight's Children* that the opening episodes of this book are very different from those of its predecessor. In each case, though for different reasons, Saleem's spurious lineage and Omar Khayyam's childhood seem to be only tenuously relevant to the remainder of the story. But the claustrophobia of the latter contrasts strongly with the wide-ranging, forward-looking anticipation aroused by the former.

Omar Khayyam makes his first contact with the outside world through a telescope, thus establishing his frequently emphasized role throughout the novel as a voyeur. He also explores his grandfather's library, teaches himself several languages, reads widely in history, literature, and travel books, and learns how to hypnotize the family servants from Mesmer's treatise on the subject. Later, having tricked his mothers into giving him his liberty and sending him to school, he uses this skill to seduce the hitherto scornful Farah Zoroaster, whose charms first captivate him through a telescope. Eventually he goes to medical school, becomes a doctor, and disappears from the story for several chapters.

Next, in an India in the shadow of prepartition riots, we meet Bilquis Kemal, about to be orphaned by a bomb exploding in the cinema managed by her father, who is quixotically flaunting his religious tolerance by showing a double bill of movies equally objectionable in the one case to Hindus and the other to Moslems. The searing blast of the explosion strips her of all but a fragment of her clothes, but when she comes to in the Red Fort, a refuge set aside for Muslims during the riots, she is wrapped in an officer's coat. Its owner, Captain Raza Hyder, proceeds to clothe her by presenting her with a new item of apparel each time he visits her, and then he marries her in order to reverse the procedure.

Thus the comic "surtext" has been added, one presumes, to the still discernible subtext of gloom and horror in this palimpsest of a novel about what Rushdie describes as a palimpsest of a nation. In the case of Pakistan, the metaphor refers to the unsuccessful attempt of its rulers to obliterate and deny the existence of all non-Moslem elements in the long, mixed, and only partially Moslem history of their share of the Indian subcontinent (91). In the case of the novel, of course, the reader is meant to remain simultaneously, if not always equally, aware of the superimposed layers of realism and fantasy, horror and comedy.

The comedy continues when Raza deposits his wife at the ancestral and very extended family residence. There she must sleep in a dormitory of women presided over by the diminutive matriarch, Bariamma, who snores with resolute circumspection until the nightly visits of an assortment of husbands are over. (The beds they find their way to in the dark may or may not be those of their respective wives, but since all is done thus in the name of modesty, there are no protests.) Bilquis's first pregnancy ends tragically when a son is stillborn, strangled by his umbilical cord. The next child, whom the parents "un-Islamically" think of as his reincarnation, turns out to be a daughter, Sufiya—or, as her mother is wont to think of and even refer to her, "Shame." Raza is promoted to colonel for the heroic role he plays in his country's defeat during the war with India over Kashmir, and mother and daughter accompany him to Q. There Raza steps from the train, arms outstretched to reassure the assembled crowd that he has come to protect them from rebellious tribesmen on the frontier, only to discover that the crowd has come to greet the film stars accompanying the handsome young manager of the town's about-to-be-opened new cinema. The tribesmen keep Raza so busy that Bilquis spends most afternoons at the cinema; we learn that Omar Khayyam has a younger brother, Babar, also of mysteriously maculate conception; Maulana Dawood, Moslem divine and implacable enemy of the Shakil sisters and their offspring, joins Raza's entourage on his return from the frontier and updates him on everything shameful that needs his attention; the handsome young manager of the cinema is accordingly murdered with barbaric savagery; Bilquis gives birth to a second daughter, Naveed ("Good News"), six weeks early and learns that she can bear no more children; Sufiya has an attack of brain fever that leaves her severely retarded; Babar joins the rebels and is killed by Raza's troops on Raza's orders. The tone is satiric, though hardly comic, when dealing with Raza's brutal suppression of frontier tribesmen or Dawood's religious fanaticism. For the most part, however, it reflects the novel's propensity to "deconstruct" the well-being of all its characters.

Omar Khayyam makes a brief appearance in Q. for Babar's funeral, but he has already reentered the story elsewhere. Rani, Raza's cousin and the girl in the next bed to Bilquis in Bariamma's dormitory, marries Iskander Harappa, the millionaire playboy whose constant and notorious companion in debauchery is Dr. Shakil. Raza and Iskander become linked in enmity as well as by marriage when Raza is publicly ridiculed and humiliated by Iskander as both pay court at a party to Pinkie Aurangzeb, their hostess and "widow-elect" of "crumbling Marshal Aurangzeb," the joint chief of staff asleep in the corner but still clutching an unspilled "brimming tumbler of whisky-soda" (111–12). That scene still has a quality of brittle comedy to it. Later, however, Iskander invites Bilquis and Raza to his country estate in an attempt at reconciliation. Their joint honor having been impugned by a reference to the above incident, however, Raza tries to expunge the shame by issuing a challenge and tethering himself to a stake all night awaiting an answer. Next morning he is approached by a servant and, bleary-eyed, fells him with a single blow. The scene is absurd, affecting, chilling, and not in the least amusing.

Shortly after this Raza falls from political favor and also finds himself in deep trouble with one of his daughters. Sufiya's three-year-old mind is keenly if inarticulately aware, within her twelve-year-old body, of what brings shame and what ought to bring shame on the family. When Pinkie Aurangzeb becomes a neighbor of the Hyders and takes to keeping turkeys, Bilquis is infuriated by the noise and attributes her husband's refusal to protest to his former fondness for Pinkie. Sufiya responds to the shame she senses in the air, and in the first of her somnambulant outbreaks of violence she escapes from the house, tears the heads off 218 offending turkeys, and then reaches "down into their bodies to draw their guts up through their necks with her tiny and weaponless hands" (150). Sufiya has discovered the source of the violence that incessant shame can provoke in the most peaceable of its victims. Thus the comic tone of much of the first half of the novel is almost irrecoverably lost. Sufiya then suffers a terrifyingly savage attack on her body by her own immune system, and immunologist Dr. Omar Khayyam Shakil, in the course of his struggle to rescue her from herself, finds himself falling grotesquely in love with this "twelve-year-old girl with a three-year-old mind, the daughter of the man who killed his brother" (153).

Seven years later it is "Good News" (Naveed) who is the source of the trouble. A marriage has been arranged between her and Haroun, the ne'er-do-well son of Iskander's cousin and bitter enemy, Little Mir. A week before the wedding Naveed discovers to her dismay that Haroun has no ambition and no particular wish to be a father. Almost simultaneously, the clairvoyant star player of the polo game she is watching, a certain Captain Talvar Ulhaq of the police, detects her distress and also "the hunger of [her] womb" (178) to bear countless children, all fathered by him, and this sudden foreknowledge makes him puff with anticipatory pride. They elope for a night, and on her return home Good News refuses to marry Haroun. Raza is dissuaded from killing his daughter in a scene just sufficiently melodramatic to remain comic and agrees to the new match. During the wedding feast, however, Sufiya once again detects a source of shame to her family and, launching her diminutive self at the new bridegroom, all but twists his head off—as if he were a mere turkey—before being forcibly restrained by no fewer than five people. The incident helps Raza see the wisdom of having Dr. Shakil as his other son-in-law and resident husband-physician to Sufiya, on condition that he not remove his bride from under the paternal roof without prior permission.

In the meantime, Iskander, on hearing that his cousin Little Mir has been given a post in the cabinet, changes his life-style overnight. He refuses to see either Pinkie Aurangzeb or Omar Khayyam again (his rejection of the latter reads like a parody of the newly crowned Henry V rejecting Falstaff), and he enters politics with predictably meteoric success. His party wins the next election and he becomes prime minister, rescuing Raza from obscurity and near disgrace to make him his commander-in-chief. He calculates that a combination of gratitude and stupidity at the top will ensure his immunity from any coup d'état by the armed forces.

As the reader already knows from the history Rushdie is parodying, however, Iskander is wrong. Despite the continued popularity with the masses that ensures his victory in the next election, Iskander has made too many influential enemies to be allowed to remain in power. Somewhat to his surprise, Raza finds himself heading the coup that overthrows Iskander and convicts him not only of gerrymandering an election so as to defeat his equally corrupt accusers, but also of complicity in the murder of Little Mir. For the latter offense he is condemned to death. Raza assumes power with becoming diffidence and promises to hold new elections within ninety days. As the months pass, however, the meaning of his self-awarded acronymic status of "C.M.L.A." is changed, in popular usage, from "Chief Martial Law Administrator" to *"Cancel My Last Announcement"* (250)—especially the one concerning elections. His power and his corruption become increasingly absolute.

In many ways, however, things do not go well for Raza. His spiritual adviser, Maulana Dawood, dies, and Raza is plagued thenceforward by his spirit and Iskander's whispering in his right and left ears, respectively, like good and bad angels. Talvar Ulhaq, whose clairvoyance proves invaluable by enabling him to arrest and imprison traitors before they actually commit their treason (and thereby to save their lives), is equally prescient with respect to Good News's fertility. She bears him, in quick succession, twins, triplets, quadruplets, and so on in strict arithmetic progression, till she hangs herself on the second attempt (the rope broke on the first) while pregnant for the eighth time. As Rushdie satirizes the overweening chauvinism of a man who "came to her once a year and ordered her to get ready because it was time to plant the seed, until she felt like a vegetable patch whose naturally fertile soil was being worn out by an overzealous gardener" (228), the tone of the novel becomes a particularly brutal combination of magic realism and grotesque humor. Bilquis in the meantime spends all her days making shrouds. And Sufiya?

Sufiya sleeps alone while her ayah, Shahbanou, protectively takes her place in Omar Khayyam's bed. But Sufiya knows that there is something going on that she doesn't know about, that something is happening when she hears "his grunts, her birdlike cries" (241) from his room at night—

some wifely function that, to her shame, Shahbanou must perform for her. Eventually four adolescent male villagers are found with their heads torn off and traces of semen on their clothing. Talvar Ulhaq tries to warn Raza of his sense that Sufiya is responsible, but when her father searches her room and finds a bloodstained shroud, he burns it and refuses to take heed. Later she almost kills Omar Khayyam, and consequently she is perpetually sedated and chained to a bed in the attic. Eventually, however, she escapes—leaving, like a cartoon character, a Sufiya-shaped hole behind her in the bricked-up window.

That last detail may perhaps be viewed as a horrifying parody of the comic. But the novel still has flashes of genuine comedy or comic satire. Raza, for instance, loses 111 wrestling matches and two upper central incisors in the process of restoring the army's shattered self-confidence after it loses Bangladesh. Three generals emerge "from the President's office wearing identical expressions of slightly stunned beatitude" after an hour and a half of forehead-to-prayer-mat gratitude to Allah for the Russian invasion of Afghanistan. This lucky event will, of course, ensure America's footing the bill for "about five billion dollars' worth of new military equipment" (282). But as Sufiya, murdering as she goes, approaches the capital, drawing the noose of violence tighter and tighter around it, and as angry crowds surround the president's house, the tone of the novel Rushdie refers to as "a fairy tale" becomes that of the grimmest and most retributive of such stories. Finally Raza, Bilquis, and Omar Khayyam make their escape wearing three of Bilquis's shrouds. Omar Khayyam leads them to Nishapur, where Bilquis dies of fever, the three sisters exact grim revenge on Raza for Babar's death, and Sufiya finally catches up with her husband. Rushdie admits yet again, as he imposes closure, "I'm only telling a fairy-story. My dictator will be toppled by goblinish, faery means. 'Makes it pretty easy for you,' is the obvious criticism; and I agree, I agree. But add, even if it does sound a little peevish: '*You* try and get rid of a dictator some time'" (284). Fantasy can sometimes serve to emphasize the stubborn durability of reality.

The Narrative Voice

As noted above, Rushdie acknowledges almost from the start that what he is writing is "a sort of modern fairy-tale" (72). Or, putting things another way, he explains that "the country in this story is not Pakistan, or not quite. There are two countries, real and fictional, occupying the same space, or almost the same space. My story, my fictional country exist, like myself, at a slight angle to reality" (23–24). Such insistence on the fictive nature of what he writes and writes about can take much less obtrusive forms, of course. As Timothy Brennan has pointed out, the fictional names of people and places in the book are a jumbled collection of historical and geographical names associated with the novel's locale. Thus, *Iskander* is a variation on *Alexander* (note how, in the chapter entitled "Alexander the Great," Rani's shawls are collectively entitled "The Shamelessness of Iskander the Great" [210]). Thus, *Harappa* recalls the ancient Harappan civilization of the Indus Valley, and *Mohenjo* is the name of both the Harappa country estate and the most famous Harappan archeological site. Thus, *Babar* and *Aurangzeb* are the names of the first and last great Mughal emperors, *Omar Khayyam* is named after the Persian poet best known in the West, and *Zoroaster* is the name of a Persian religious teacher and founder of Zoroastrianism, a Persian monotheistic faith. *Sufiya* is presumably derived from the Moslem mystics known as *Sufis,* and *Raza* is an alternative form of *Raja.*[4] Although the juxtapositions are in most cases satirically indicative of a sad decline from the originals, they also emphasize "the angle to reality" of Rushdie's fiction.

Such a distinction is also emphasized through the use of historical characters' actual names when they are referred to in some intrusive comment by the narrator and the use of fictional names for what are clearly their fictional counterparts. Thus "President Ayub Khan" of page 72 and "General Ayub Khan" of a joke the narrator heard on his last visit to Pakistan (120) have been promoted and abridged to "the President, Field-Marshal Mohammad A." by page 128. This transformation is scarcely more of a disguise than referring to the town of Quetta as the town of Q. But the same joke also concerns (and names) Zulfikar Ali Bhutto and General Zia, elsewhere known by their fictional sobriquets of Iskander Harappa and Raza Hyder. At one point Rushdie even considers borrowing General Napier's Latin pun and calling Pakistan "Peccavistan" (92–93).

Brennan also reports that "in interviews, Rushdie has insisted that the narrative asides of *Shame.* . . . are the would-be transcriptions of an oral tale," and he argues that this is one of the ways in which *Shame* resembles the divinely dictated, angelically recited Qur'an.[5] Similarly, Bilquis must listen while Bariamma recites such scriptural staples as genealogies, together with "family tales. . . . lurid affairs, featuring divorces, bankruptcies, droughts, cheating friends, child mortality, diseases of the breast, men cut down in their prime, failed hopes, lost beauty, women who grew obscenely fat, smuggling deals, opium-taking poets, pining virgins, curses, typhoid, bandits, homosexuality, sterility, frigidity, rape, the high price of food, gamblers, drunks, murders, suicides and God" (78–79). Already the catalogue of disparate disasters reads like a parody of a Rushdie novel. But "Bariamma's mildly droning recital of family horrors had the effect somehow of defusing them, making them safe, embalming them in the mummifying fluid of her own incontrovertible respectability" (79). When Bilquis listens to her own story, which "altered, at first, in the retellings, but finally . . . settled down, and after that nobody, neither teller nor listener, would tolerate any deviation from the hallowed, sacred text" (79), we see the mechanism of scripturalizing at work. Playfully, unobtrusively, but undeniably, Rushdie has not only insisted on the fallibly fictional status of his novel but also anticipated *The Satanic Verses* by implying the fallibly human processes by which all "hallowed, sacred text[s]" are arrived at and sanctified.

Another way in which Rushdie reminds his readers, even more comprehensively than Saleem does in *Midnight's Children,* that what they are reading is fictional is by foreshadowing and demonstrating complete control over future developments and events. Perhaps the most extensive example of this occurs soon after Bilquis enters the story.

I am wondering how best to describe Bilquis. As a woman who was unclothed by change, but who wrapped herself in certainties; or as a girl who became a queen, but lost the ability possessed by every beggar-woman, that is, the power of bearing sons; or as that lady whose father was a Woman and whose son turned out to be a girl as well; and whose man of men, her Razzoo or Raz-Matazz, was himself obliged to put on the humiliating black shroud of womanhood; or perhaps as a being in the secret grip of fate—for did not the umbilical noose that stifled her son find its echo, or twin, in another and more terrible rope? (69)

In addition to such titillation of the reader's Padma-like "what-happened-nextism," moreover, *Shame* includes and makes use of much more explicit and detailed references to key historical-fictional events to come. On page 115, for instance, just before Raza hitches himself to a post at Mohenjo for the night, we read: "After the death of Isky Harappa, Rani and Arjumand Harappa were kept locked up in Mohenjo for several years, and to fill the silences the mother told the daughter about the shawl." Then, on page 204, we are told: "They hanged him in the middle of the night," and learn, over the next ten pages, how Rani discovers that her husband has been shot before being hanged, how mother and daughter torment their jailer, and how the shawls Rani embroiders tell the story of Iskander's years in power. Finally, in the chapter "Monologue of a Hanged Man," interleaved with the details (also referred to more than once earlier in the book) of the discovery of Sufiya's bestial nature, of her "madwoman-in-the-attic" imprisonment, and of her escape, we have the full details of Iskander's arrest, imprisonment, murder, and fake execution. These latter details are perhaps the most intriguing and controversial of the novel's fictionalized "facts." Moreover, it is precisely with respect to these events that Rushdie is insisting—both by treating their sequence so cavalierly and by switching back and forth between the final "authoritative" version of the story and some of the most unequivocal and symbolic fantasy in the book—that he is in charge, that this is *his* version of events.

Clearly the novel lacks the involution of *Midnight's Children*, or of André Gide's *Les faux-monnayeurs* (*The Counterfeiters*) and Vladimir Nabokov's *Pale Fire*. In such works the self-reflexive element (i.e., the capacity of the novel, and also its apparent need, to insist on and analyze its own fictive nature) is so integrally a part of the fiction that it even calls itself into question. *Shame*, by contrast, establishes its narrator as someone quite distinct from the action of the novel, someone in the "real" world, of which the novel is a mimesis—someone, in short, who knows Ali Bhutto as Ali Bhutto in the real world and as Iskander Harappa in the reflected world of the novel, whereas Raza Hyder knows him only as Iskander Harappa. In this sense of standing back or apart from the novel, Rushdie has a relationship to *Shame* not unlike that of Thackeray to *Vanity Fair*. He disclaims any knowledge, when it suits him, as to what makes Omar Khayyam fall in love with Sufiya (153–56, 218), just as Thackeray, when it suits him, denies knowing why Becky Sharp behaves as she does. Yet clearly Rushdie is as firmly in charge of his puppets and their behavior as Thackeray was. He even says of Sufiya's retardation: "I did it to her, I think, to make her pure. Couldn't think of another way of creating purity in what is supposed to be the Land of the Pure . . . and idiots are, by definition, innocent" (129). Unlike Saleem, moreover, whose readers know him to be a fiction, Rushdie is his readers' only and ultimate source of information and must retain their faith in his reliability if he is to suspend their disbelief.

That the narrator is in charge and has designs on the reader, and that author and narrator are identical, is most evident when, in what is clearly a very personal statement, Rushdie recounts the origins of *Shame* as being three incidents he read about in London.[6] In the first, an immigrant Pakistani father "murdered his only child, a daughter, because by making love to a white boy she brought such dishonour upon her family that only her blood could wash away the stain" (123). In the second, a girl is "set upon in a late night underground train by a group of teenage boys. . . . The girl 'Asian' again, the boys predictably white. Afterwards, remembering her

beating, she feels not angry but ashamed" (125). In the third, a boy is
found "blazing in a parking lot. . . . and the experts who examined his body
and the scene of the incident were forced to accept what seemed impossible:
namely that the boy had simply ignited of his own accord" (126). Of the
first incident Rushdie reports that he found himself sympathizing with the
father. He did so with great difficulty, with horror even, having just become
a father himself, but with empathy—in a way those brought up in a culture
where such compelling shame is unknown may find impossible. Of the second he found himself fantasizing what might have happened if the weak,
defenseless girl had suddenly rounded on her attackers with superhuman
strength. In such a way, sometimes, oppressed minorities riot, set fire to
shops, overturn cars. "Humiliate people for long enough and a wildness
bursts out" (125).

The relevance of the second case to that of Sufiya is blazingly obvious,
and it also anticipates important aspects of *The Satanic Verses*. The third incident, though Rushdie offers no comment, is reflected in Sufiya's capacity
to blush with magical fierceness, almost from birth, at both her own shame
and what should have been the shame of others. As to the first incident,
Rushdie was presumably moved by the way it enabled him to empathize
with shame of an intensity, though not of a kind, that one is the poorer for
not being able to feel. The point at issue here, however, is not the nature of
the messages Rushdie received from these incidents and sets out to convey in
the novel; what is important is the fact that he does set out—and even acknowledges that he sets out—to convey certain messages. Perhaps Brecht is
a better analogy than Thackeray, with Rushdie's frank acknowledgment of
the fictive—indeed, the didactively fictive—nature of what he writes being
the equivalent of Brechtian alienation.

It should already be clear that there is no pretense in this novel that author and narrator are other than one and the same. Insertions of the first
person, such as "But I have been out of doors for quite long enough now,
and must get my narrative out of the sun before it is affected by mirages or
heatstroke" (18) or "on my way back to the story, I pass Omar Khayyam
Shakil, my sidelined hero, who is waiting patiently for me to get to the
point at which his future bride, poor Sufiya Zinobia, can enter the narrative,
headfirst down the birth canal" (73), can be dismissed as playful parodies of
nineteenth-century metafictional naïvetés, such as "And now, dear readers,
it is time. . . ." Even admonitions such as "Do not form too low an opinion
of Atiyah [Pinkie] Aurangzeb" (114) need not strip Rushdie of that protective "persona" with which scholars seek to equip even the author of "Tintern
Abbey" when talking "first to himself, then to his sister."[7] But when

Rushdie informs his readers that "a few weeks after Russian troops entered Afghanistan, I returned home, to visit my parents and sisters and to show off my firstborn son" (20), his intention is surely to lay unequivocal claim to the narrative voice as being his own. Both the claim and his reason for making it become clearer still when he adds: "My story, my fictional country exist, like myself, at a slight angle to reality. I have found this off-centering to be necessary; but its value is, of course, open to debate. My view is that I am not writing only about Pakistan" (24). The fact that he is not writing *only* about Pakistan implies that his subject includes Pakistan—that is, Pakistan as a political entity—but also extends to anywhere else the cap is perceived to fit. From the phrases "my story," "my fictional country," and "my view" readers may assume that Rushdie has no wish to hide behind any assumption that the voice speaking is that of a persona. This is his view of his subject expressed in his voice.

I suggested, in my concluding remarks about *Midnight's Children*, that the first-person narration by Saleem was a kind of apprenticeship during which Rushdie tested both the potential and the limitations, the reliability and the fallibility, of his chosen medium of fiction. I even implied that only then was he ready to write *Shame*, and the contrast between *Midnight's Children* and *Shame* is marked. No longer are we playing games with a narrator of great charm but dubious reliability. It is all too clear who and what is being satirized, who and what we are to disapprove of, and such force and clarity are due in no small part to the narrator's first-person interpolations. "Since my last visit to Karachi," he writes, for instance, "my friend the poet had spent many months in jail, for social reasons. That is to say, he knew somebody who knew somebody who was the wife of the second cousin by marriage of the step-uncle of somebody who might or might not have shared a flat with someone who was running guns to the guerrillas in Baluchistan" (22).

There are, however, other occasions—occasions such as the discussion arising out of a performance of *Danton's Death*—when Rushdie wishes to wear his philosophical hat and argue that members of the cast of that or any play or the play of life are never wholly at one extreme or the other of the many dichotomies or polarities into which one can choose to divide people—that we are all part Danton and part Robespierre and that life is always a medley of grays (265–67). When Saleem indulges in such pontifications in *Midnight's Children*, the reader is usually invited to take them with a pinch of irony. By choosing to speak so clearly and confidently in his own voice in *Shame*, however, Rushdie exposes himself to the danger of taking himself more seriously than he would a surrogate.

Cohesion

As already noted, a controlling and paradoxically unifying image right from the start of *Midnight's Children* is that of Aadam Aziz falling in love with his wife-to-be (almost as if from the blurred snapshot of a mail-order bride) by assembling a series of fragments each seven inches in diameter. This image becomes a metaphor, of course, for the way in which the narrator assembles the story from fragments, which in turn expresses the author's sense of how human perception pieces together as much as it can of an overall concept of the nature of life. Almost equally early in *Shame* there is an apparently equivalent image of fragmentation when Omar Khayyam visits Farah Zoroaster's home at the frontier post between Pakistan and Iran. Broken pieces of mirror have been tied to the posts marking the frontier, and "as Farah approaches each fragment she sees shards of herself reflected in the glass, and smiles her private smile." Recognizing that she is far too self-absorbed to be won by conventional means, he asks her if she has ever been hypnotized, and "for the first time in history, she looks at him with interest" (50).

Rushdie uses the same image in a paper he read at a seminar in 1982. *Shame* had not yet been published, though Farah's seduction had perhaps already been consummated in manuscript. "The broken mirror may actually be as valuable as the one which is supposedly unflawed," Rushdie argues in describing the process of recreating "the Bombay of the 1950s and 1960s" in memory before beginning to write *Midnight's Children,* and he continues by insisting that "it was precisely the partial nature of these memories, their fragmentation, that made them so evocative for me. The shards of memory acquired greater status, greater resonance because they were *remains;* fragmentation made trivial things seem like symbols, and the mundane acquired numinous qualities. There is an obvious parallel here with archeology. The broken pots of antiquity . . . are exciting to discover, even if they are pieces of the most quotidian objects."[8]

In *Midnight's Children,* it seems, Rushdie would have us see fragmentation as an inescapable feature of the human condition, whether inherent in the nature of things or merely in our perception of them, and as such to be endured and coped with as best we can. In remembering how he went about recreating Bombay in memory, he elevates fragmentation so as to become a feature of the creative process—a positive asset. But in *Shame* fragmentation is given an immediate narcissistic role and thereby serves notice that Farah typifies most of the other characters in the novel. In this way the image of mirror fragments sets the tone for the book as a whole, in that its implications are neither ontological nor psychological nor even stylistic, but strictly satiric; like it or not, this is how people are—addicted to mirrors.

Of the other factors lending *Midnight's Children* such unity as it possesses, the most important is the way its numerous and varied dramatis personae are linked by an essentially picaresque narrative structure. In the case of *Shame,* however, there is no single, dominant character for unity to derive from. Coincidence and family links provide a loose framework within which the characters combine to create a tight satiric pattern. Raza and Iskander, for instance, are compared and contrasted throughout in their rivalry, and they demonstrate the potentially equal dangers of stupidity and intelligence when combined with ambition. Bilquis and Rani resemble and differ from one another in their wifely eclipses and their final wifely offerings of shawls and shrouds. Naveed and Arjumand meet with equal disillusion in their search for fulfillment through a man, whether husband or father. And Omar Khayyam is the perpetual onlooker—not the wise bystander who sees more of the game than the players, but the voyeur, the passive confidant in turn of Iskander and Raza, the "done-to" rather than the "doer." That he is paired with Sufiya underlines her even more passive role for much of the book, though that it should be he rather than Raza or Rani whom she finally beheads distinguishes his passivity from hers. They may be the "Mr. and Mrs. Everyone" of the book, but they fulfill these roles in different ways. He is the guilty party as everyone is at times by association, by his or her condoning acquiescence, whereas she is the innocent victim as everyone is at times by association, by merely being there. Finally, Chhunni, Munnee, and Bunny, like the three fates, are the alpha and omega of it all.

In a similar way the magic of the book is distributed among a number of characters rather than being concentrated in one, and it is functional in a far more strictly satiric way than the magic in *Midnight's Children.* Most obviously satiric is Talvar Ulhaq's clairvoyance, which "made it possible for him to arrest a future traitor before he committed his act of treason, and thus save the fellow's life" (184). Equally if less amusingly satiric is his ability to "plant the seed" annually from which would grow Naveed's progressively abundant harvests. The supernatural transformation of Babar into an angel is in obviously comic contrast to the diabolic propensities of Raza and Omar Khayyam. And of the two sisters, indeed of all the women in the book, Sufiya is certainly the key one to suffer from oppression, though far from the only one. Both her blushing, intensifying from her birth onward till her bathwater could scald her ayah's hands (121), and the subsequent growing power of the beast within her are magical symbols of all that the title of the novel and the use of that same word more than a hundred times in the text stand for.

The remaining example of magic is the triple pregnancy of the three sisters. This device functions less to satirize than to set Omar Khayyam apart from his fellow men. To have Chhunni, Munnee, and Bunny join forces with Sufiya at the end, however, as she topples a dictatorship by "goblinish, faery means," not only completes the magic circle by letting the story end where it begins but also emphasizes that to achieve as much in real life is another matter altogether.

Sufiya and "Shame"

The final element contributing to the cohesion of the book and helping to express its anger is closely associated with Sufiya—it is in fact the disease from which she is suffering or, rather, the scientific concept that helps us to diagnose a number of diseases, including Sufiya's fictional one. Even had Hugh Everett's "many worlds" hypothesis informed *Grimus,* the role of the immune-system hypothesis in *Shame* would still have been far more central and important—more so even than that of the pickling process in *Midnight's Children.* But first we should look at all the women characters in *Shame* and in that way begin by locating Sufiya within a context rather than regarding her as a freak. Whether we agree with it or not, Rushdie's own assessment of the role played by his women characters in *Shame* is the obvious place to begin.

Once upon a time there were two families, their destinies inseparable even by death. I had thought, before I began, that what I had on my hands was an almost excessively masculine tale, a saga of sexual rivalry, ambition, power, patronage, betrayal, death, revenge. But the women seem to have taken over; they marched in from the peripheries of the story to demand the inclusion of their own tragedies, histories and comedies, obliging me to couch my narrative in all manner of sinuous complexities, to see my "male" plot refracted, so to speak, through the prisms of its reverse and "female" side. It occurs to me that the women knew precisely what they were up to—that their stories explain, and even subsume, the men's. Repression is a seamless garment; a society which is authoritarian in its social and sexual codes, which crushes its women beneath the intolerable burdens of honour and propriety, breeds repressions of other kinds as well. Contrariwise: dictators are always—or at least in public, on other people's behalf—puritanical. So it turns out that my "male" and "female" plots are the same story, after all. (189)

Clearly Rushdie wishes to add support for feminism to his other "liberal" attitudes. As already noted, the treatment meted out to Naveed by her strutting parody of a philoprogenitive husband is grotesquely chauvinistic. Iskander's behavior too, whether in the pornographic perversions of his playboy days, his village of kept white women, or his almost total neglect of Rani until he needs her at his side to complete the image he wishes to present to the electorate, is a model of male exploitiveness—all the more credible for being less fantastic than Talvar Ulhaq's. Although far more ridiculous in the way it is presented, Raza's desperate need to have a son is at least as far-reaching in its consequences. The scene in the hospital—when it takes the medical supervisor, a brigadier, to come to the rescue of the midwife and outrank Major Hyder before the latter will believe that his child is beyond doubt a daughter—uses ridicule to satirize and yet at the same time to help the reader understand the intensity of this culturally imposed preference. Raza's rage communicates itself, moreover, not only to the agitated mother but also to the child in her arms, who begins to blush. From the start Sufiya is acquainted with shame.

However, if Raza or the male dominance that he embodies in this instance is initially responsible for the shame felt by Sufiya, it must be admitted that Bilquis continues to instill it in a far more sustained manner. From the outset she sees Sufiya's brain fever and subsequent retardation as a "judgment" on her cinematic adultery and as her "shame" (106–107). Rushdie emphasizes this connection, moreover, by using the slowness of Sufiya's mental growth as a symbol of her innocence and as the occasion for an unusually poetic passage. "See how, growing, she caresses a pebble in her hand, unable to say why goodness seems to lie within this smooth flat stone; how she glows with pleasure when she hears loving words, even though they are almost always meant for someone else." The characters used as foils for such innocence, moreover, and for whom she in turn acts as a foil, are her mother and sister. "Bilquis," writes Rushdie, "poured all her affection over her younger daughter, Naveed. 'Good News'—the nickname had stuck, like a pulled face in the wind—was soaked in it, a monsoon of love, while Sufiya Zinobia, her parents' burden, her mother's shame, remained as dry as the desert" (129–30). Of Naveed he claims that "you could have taken the whole quantity of sisterly love inside Good News Hyder, sealed it in an envelope and posted it anywhere in the world for one rupee airmail, that's how much it weighed" (148).[9] But of Sufiya, her mother having hacked her hair off in maternal rage as she slept amid the corpses of turkeys, he says: "She was taken to hospital with pus bursting from her sores, dribbling, incontinent, with the rough, cropped proof of her mother's loathing on her head" (152). Raza, on the other hand, develops a protective tenderness toward his elder daughter from this point in the story onward.

Thus, however Rushdie may protest, his women characters are not exempt from being sources of shame. Moreover, though the shortcomings of an Iskander or a Raza, to say nothing of those of a Talvar Ulhaq, are shown as comfortably exceeding in scope those of all the women put together, men as a gender are not subjected to such sweeping sexist stereotyping as: "at the time of the Pan-Islamic conference when Heads of State arrived from all over the globe . . . they all brought their mothers along, so that all hell broke loose, because the mothers in the zenana wing embarked at once on a tooth-and-nail struggle for seniority, and they kept sending urgent messages to their sons, interrupting the conference's plenipotentiary sessions to complain about mortal insults received and honour besmirched, which brought the world leaders close to starting fist-fights or even wars" (272–73).

As personalities in their own right the women tend to be less idiosyncratically interesting than characters such as Naseem the "whatsitsname" Reverend Mother, or Amina with her racecourse winnings and innocently silent assignations with her former husband, or above all Padma, in *Midnight's Children.* Like everything else in *Shame,* they are much more tightly subject to the overall satiric nature of the work. In general this satiric purpose requires them to be victims; only in the fairy-tale ending are Chhunni, Munnee, Bunny, and Sufiya able to turn the tables on their male oppressors. Moreover, being a victim for Sufiya involves violence of a horrifyingly self-destructive kind.

In the first place, and on a psychologically realistic plane, we are presumably to see this rejection of Sufiya by her own defense forces, as if her whole body were a gigantic transplant, as a psychosomatic enactment of the lack of self-esteem, the self-loathing even, felt by a child so fiercely rejected by her mother. On a more figurative level, Rushdie presents this illness as the self-destructive outcome of her having taken unto herself all the shame that belonged to others but that they disavowed: "the unfelt shame of those around her, for instance what had not been felt by Raza Hyder when he gunned down Babar Shakil—as well as the increasing shame of her own existence, and of her hacked off hair" (141). Sufiya the married woman even feels shame that her ayah must play the nightly role of wife to Omar Khayyam. But she also sees strange pictures among memories of "herself with dead birds" or of "biting someone"—pictures "that don't seem to be from anywhere. . . . with people hanging upside-down from the roof" (236). These latter images clearly allude to earlier descriptions of political persecution (22) of which Sufiya is totally unaware—in other words, to sins and suffering of which she knows nothing but must bear the shame. In answer to his own question, "What is a saint?", Rushdie replies, "A saint is a person who suffers in our stead" (153). As Rushdie is a lapsed Muslim, however, we are spared having to see Sufiya as a Christ figure. The capacity for violence that, after the slaughtering and gutting of Pinkie's turkeys, all but destroys her own body, is redirected outward. First there is the ritual beheading and evisceration of four village youths, then similar nationwide "murders of animals and men" (280), and finally the annihilation of her husband, of Raza Hyder, and of Raza's regime. In this way Rushdie turns her into a symbol of the retributive capacity of the downtrodden finally to turn the tables on their oppressors. Her magical folktale powers are a single, negative equivalent of the rich variety of powers displayed by the children of midnight, and as such, paradoxically, they constitute the single note of hope in the novel.

Considered as a structural element within the novel, Sufiya's self-rejection is important as something that is echoed by rejection after rejection elsewhere. Examples abound: the east and west wings of the country reject each other; secessionists in Baluchistan reject and are rejected by the central government; Ayub Khan, Shaggy Dog, Iskander Harappa, and Raza Hyder are rejected in turn by the country they rule; Sufiya is rejected by Bilquis; Raza is rejected by Pinkie Aurangzeb; Rani and Pinkie are rejected by Iskander; Haroun is rejected by Naveed; Arjumand is rejected by Haroun; Farah Zoroaster rejects both Omar Khayyam and Eduardo; and Omar Khayyam is also rejected by Babar, Iskander, and finally Sufiya. Who, in fact, is accepting of anyone without reservation except Shahbanou of Sufiya, and just possibly Arjumand of her father?

Finally, there is the rejection of a body by its own defenders as metaphor—the treason of those whom the body most trusts and depends on for its health and the corruption there must be in high places for such a thing to happen. It is impossible not to think of such a disease in political terms. So one has only to sense how intimately terrifying and humiliating it must be to suffer from such a complaint for the strength of the metaphor, when reversed and applied to the body politic, to become apparent. Throughout the novel just such treachery is taking place throughout Rushdie's fictional Pakistan—just such self-rejection. The whole atmosphere in *Shame* is thus the antithesis of the inclusiveness that characterizes most of *Midnight's Children*. From the multiple, muddled, all-embracing world of a thousand and one stories about a thousand and one children, of a narrator who claims to be a swallower of lives that readers too must swallow in order to know him, of narrative seen as a pickling process each one of whose pickle jars "contains . . . the most exalted of possibilities: the feasibility of the chutnification of history" (*M.C.,* 442)—that is, from an inclusive Hindu world—we have moved to the embittered, rejecting world of Islam.

Chapter Six
The Satanic Verses

After the very limited recognition accorded *Grimus,* for Rushdie to spend six years writing and rewriting *Midnight's Children,* and in the process to expand the scope and extend the stylistic range of his fiction in ways few readers of that earlier novel could have predicted, must have taken tremendous self-confidence and courage. First novels that have such modest success are seldom followed up by second ones of such ambitious size and with such innovatively complex treatment of unfamiliar subject matter. The making of *Shame,* by contrast, was a kind of consolidation—a reuse and a refining, in a smaller and much more focused work completed within a mere two years, of techniques first developed in *Midnight's Children.* It was merely short-listed, moreover, for the Booker Prize. So when it took an additional five years for his next novel, *The Satanic Verses,* to appear, no one was surprised that it was longer and in many respects more ambitious and innovative in form than *Midnight's Children.* It was also even more all-inclusive in that, though most of the action takes place in London, episodes ranging in length from whole sections or books to brief incidents are located in the Middle East (and/or the dreams of one of the characters), India, Scotland, and New York, as well as in both the seventh and twentieth centuries. As Rushdie himself, while still writing *Shame,* said of the direction his fiction would take in the future: "At some point the writing is going to perform the same migration that I did. Because otherwise it becomes spurious to spend your life living in the West and writing exotically about far distant lands, maharajahs . . . I am very interested in writing about the idea of migration and the effect it has on individuals and groups. And somewhere, I think, there's an enormous novel waiting to be written, unfortunately . . ."[1] Moreover, despite the becoming modesty of "unfortunately," it is clear in hindsight that Rushdie was eager for new fields to conquer and confident to the point of recklessness in his ability to succeed.

As Rushdie foresaw would be the case, the novel breaks new ground by being set mainly in London, his new home. The city the novel describes, moreover, has become home to a whole new immigrant population and seems almost as remote and exotic and unexplored by English fiction as the India and Pakistan of Rushdie's previous two novels. It is equally unexplored, one is tempted to add, by the social and intellectual world in which Rushdie, as a member of England's literati, was living while writing the novel. With his usual eye for color and ear for the nuances of language, however, Rushdie captures a spirited simulacrum of the world of the immigrant—along with that inhabited by advertising executives, actors, and other self-promoters like Rushdie himself—that in many ways is closer to its essence than more grittily realistic studies. Above all, Rushdie uses his version of the immigrant world in his own inimitable way.

A further and, as things have transpired, tragically crucial difference between this novel and its precursors is the sequence of dreams that alternate with ongoing events in the main story line and in which one of the two actor protagonists dreams he is the Archangel Gibreel (i.e., Gabriel) in episodes from the lives of the Prophet Muhammad and lesser, later figures. On a first reading many readers may remain unconvinced that these dream episodes are an integral or essential part of the novel, despite its title, and it is important that this study examine the issue along with the whole question of the response of Islam to that portion of the novel.

Metamorphoses

Gibreel Farishta and Saladin Chamcha, the only survivors of an Air India jumbo jet held to ransom for 110 days and finally blown up over the English Channel by Sikh terrorists, fall to earth unharmed, embracing each other "head-to-tail" and "performing their geminate cartwheels all the way down." In doing so they pass through "a succession of cloudforms, ceaselessly metamorphosing, gods into bulls, women into spiders, men into wolves. . . . and Chamcha . . . was seized by the notion that he, too, had acquired the quality of cloudiness, becoming metamorphic, hybrid. . . ."[2]

Introduced thus in middescent and *medias res* to the novel's twin protagonists and to a recurring tendency of theirs and of the things, people, beliefs around them to metamorphose, we are subsequently informed briefly of their life histories to date. Gibreel was born near Bombay of poor parents, orphaned young, and adopted by an employer who engineered an opening for him in the film industry. Early in life he became fascinated by religion and mythology, "devouring the metamorphic myths of Greece and Rome, the avatars of Jupiter, the boy who became a flower, the spider-woman, Circe, everything," as well as dubiously authentic accounts (as Rushdie adds, deconstructing before the event) of the satanic verses episode that provides the novel with its title and much else (23–24). Then, with the coming of the theological movies retelling the stories of Hinduism, he was given his big break in six movies as the elephant-headed god, Ganesh, and in an adventure series as Hanuman the monkey god, after which even the sky was scarcely a limit. Clearly the metamorphosis every actor experiences temporarily with each new part is magnified when the role is that of a deity, especially that of metamorphic Vishnu or one of his avatars. Shortly before the opening episode of the novel, however, Gibreel, like Aadam Aziz at the outset of *Midnight's Children,* suffers a lapse of his Islamic faith. As a guilty consequence, he is afflicted whenever he sleeps by end-to-end dreams in which he becomes the Archangel Gibreel, and therefore he tries to sleep as little and as seldom as possible. Saladin Chamcha on the other hand, like Rushdie himself, is the son of a wealthy Bombay businessman who sent his son to be educated at boarding school and university in England. Father and son quarreled bitterly, so Saladin settled in England, strove to metamorphose into someone more English than the English, and married a woman he judged to be the epitome of the English upper classes without realizing that she was marrying him to escape from that very stereotype. He too became an actor—"the Man of a Thousand Voices and a Voice," able to play all thirty-seven roles in a radio play or be the voice-over for a ketchup bottle, a packet of garlic-flavored chips, or a roll of carpet in a television commercial (60). His metamorphoses may have been less profound than Gibreel's, but they were much more prolific. In all of them, however, he was invisible to his audience. So his most ardently sought-after metamorphosis, into a bona fide English butterfly, was less than a total success.

Within an Indian context, of course, the most radical yet also the most everyday kind of metamorphosis is reincarnation. And the first words in the book, spoken or rather sung by Gibreel, are: "To be born again, first you have to die"—words repeated or echoed throughout the book. Once the two men are safely on land, moreover, the closing words of the first chapter are to the effect that Saladin Chamcha coughed and spluttered and, "as befitted a new-born babe, burst into foolish tears" (10). Nor are such words to be taken lightly. For the whole novel centers around a change, a metamorphosis, a rebirth that both survivors undergo during a descent that should result in death but that miraculously leaves them both alive, though changed. Within hours of his landing Gibreel Farishta develops a halo worthy of his archangelic namesake. And within hours of his fall Saladin Chamcha begins to grow horns, which are followed with alarming rapidity by hooves and a tail.

The two of them are first greeted by Rosa Diamond, a widow in her late eighties. But others too see them come ashore and report the fact to the police, who arrive at Rosa's house by the beach in search of illegal immigrants.

One glance at Saladin's forehead is enough to convince them of his guilt, just as one glimpse of the halo worn by Gibreel, to whom Saladin vainly turns for help, is enough to satisfy them of his irreproachability. Gibreel remains with Rosa for several days, and we are informed of her past life by the curious expedient of her reliving key episodes therefrom—episodes she shares with Gibreel in a kind of mutual waking dream. She is drawn in particular to her years as the wife of an ornithologically preoccupied Anglo-Argentinian who seems not to notice or resent the attraction between her and his chief gaucho, Martin de la Cruz, and Gibreel is helpless to prevent himself becoming Martin de la Cruz in answer to her overwhelming need. Not only is the role he must play subject to metamorphosis, however. So is the one she in fact played in these episodes. She keeps trying to decide whether she did or did not, on a certain island, allow him to—"the two possibilities kept alternating, while dying Rosa tossed on her bed, did she didn't she, making the last version of the story of her life, unable to decide what she wanted to be true"(152).

Saladin in the meantime, growing hairier and hornier by the moment, to the ribald amusement of his captors, is taken by police van to a special medical facility at the detention center for illegal immigrants, where he encounters metamorphoses on a scale and to an extent he can scarcely credit. As a kind of reverse manticore with an entirely human body but the head of a ferocious tiger and three rows of teeth explains, a woman patient is by now mostly water buffalo, businessmen from Nigeria have grown sturdy tails, and a group of holidaymakers from Senegal who were merely changing planes have been turned into slippery snakes. Asked why and how, he simply says, "They describe us . . . That's all. They have the power of description, and we succumb to the pictures they construct" (167–68). Clearly such metamorphoses are symbolic of the power of suggestion, and in particular of the way racial prejudice works like a self-fulfilling prophecy. But taken in conjunction with Rosa Diamond's control over Gibreel and her ability to reshape her own past life (and the similar control, in the actor Gibreel's dreams, that Muhammad—known in the dream as "Mahound" —exerts over the Archangel Gibreel, to say nothing of his ability to reshape incidents such as that of the satanic verses), these metamorphoses seem to imply that Rushdie considers the most important changes in people's lives to be psychological in nature, whether self-induced or imposed from outside by more "hegemonic" personalities and social pressures.

Saladin escapes as part of a mass breakout and surprises his friend Jumpy Joshi in bed with his wife, consoling her in her bereavement. Pamela Chamcha refuses to acknowledge this bedraggled, horned beast sprawled in the hallway as her husband, and the mortified friend takes the hideously transformed Saladin to the Shaandaar Café, a restaurant and rooming house run by Muhammad and Hind Sufyan, immigrants from Bangladesh. There, to the horror of Hind and the unholy delight of her two teenage daughters, Mishal and Anahita, Saladin remains holed up for the next several months and hundred and ten or so pages.

Gibreel too makes his escape from Rosa Diamond's dreams. His whole journey to England was undertaken in pursuit of Alleluia Cone, pale and blonde and beautiful, the first woman to climb Mount Everest, and Gibreel's lover for three days and nights while in India. So, evading Rosa's clutches, he falls into those of a surprised but delighted Alleluia. There he sleeps for seven days and nights in sheer exhaustion. But it is not just bad dreams or the time spent in captivity from which he needs to recover. Once their infatuation resumes, it becomes apparent that there are flaws in the relationship that neither can correct. Chief of these is Gibreel's pathological jealousy, of which hitherto he has been unaware, never having valued one woman highly enough above the rest to feel that way about her. To refer to the emotion as "pathological," moreover, is no mere figure of speech; it quickly blossoms into full-blown schizophrenic paranoia as his dreams leak into his waking life and he changes into a full-time archangel. As such he sees and submits to being chided by a bespectacled, balding God sitting on Alleluia's bed, realizes that he is being hampered in his mission to save London by something dangerously close to uxoriousness, walks out on Alleluia, makes fruitless and misunderstood attempts to help or admonish sundry citizens of London, and is knocked down by a car when trying to halt the flow of rush-hour traffic in order to make people pay attention.

The owner of the car, an Indian film producer, recognizes him, returns him to Alleluia, and helps her nurse him back to normality, only to exploit him in a gala return to a public that has given him up for dead. When he makes his entry by being lowered to the stage in a chariot, however, he reverts to his other role in life and, *angelus ex machina,* levitates from the stage unaided. Attempts are made to persuade the media that the chariot is winched back up to rescue Gibreel from fans invading the stage, but in fact it never leaves the stage. Meanwhile, high over London, Gibreel suddenly realizes that what is wrong with the city is its weather. Patently, it seems to him,

the moral fuzziness of the English was meteorologically induced. "When the day is not warmer than the night," he reasoned, "when the light is not brighter than the dark, when the land is not drier than the sea, then clearly a people will lose the

power to make distinctions, and commence to see everything—from political parties to sexual partners to religious beliefs—as much-the-same, nothing-to-choose,
give-or-take. What folly! For truth is extreme, it is *so* and not *thus,* it is *him* and not
her, a partisan matter, not a spectator sport. It is, in brief, *heated.* City," he cried,
and his voice rolled over the metropolis like thunder, "I am going to tropicalize
you." (354)

And so he does, closing his eyes as his body exudes the enormous and elemental energy needed to accomplish such a transformation, then opening
them to find himself once more on Alleluia Cone's doorstep. This passage is
a superb example of the parodies that abound in the novel. It captures not
only the total confidence with which the Imam of one of Gibreel's dreams
and so many others like him diagnose the world's ills and propose their instant remedies, but it also expresses the absolutism of fundamentalist
belief—"truth is extreme, it is *so* and not *thus,* it is *him* and not *her*"—and
transposes it all into the absurdity of London's spiritual redemption seen as
a matter of degrees, whether Fahrenheit or Celsius.

What is also at issue, however, is the distinction between magic and reality. When Gibreel and Saladin fall from 29,002 feet (the precise height of
Mount Everest) into the English Channel and are washed up on a beach
unharmed—as when subsequently Gibreel acquires an intermittent halo
and Saladin a set of horns, hooves, and a tail—we know we are in the realm
of magic. The same is true, despite its happening under medical auspices,
when a human being is made to incorporate a high proportion of water-
buffalo. In such cases we are conscious of a strongly symbolic, even a didactic intent on Rushdie's part; there is certainly no attempt to explain such
metamorphic phenomena realistically. The situation is quite different, however, when Gibreel decides that it is time to summon the citizens of London
to repentance as, standing beside the Thames, he begins to enlarge his archangelic person till it is huge enough to straddle the river.

"I am Gibreel," he shouted in a voice that shook every building on the riverbank:
nobody noticed. Not one person came running out of those quaking edifices to escape the earthquake. Blind, deaf and asleep.
    He decided to force the issue.
    The stream of traffic flowed past him. He took a mighty breath, lifted one gi-
gantic foot, and stepped out to face the cars. (336–37)

Gibreel's change in size is wholly illusory, and the function of the episode is
to illustrate his state of mind. On his next outing as the archangel, however,

strong doubts are cast on the attempt to downplay his miraculous levitation from the stage at Earls Court. While hovering over London, moreover, he tropicalizes the city's climate before landing on Alleluia's doorstep yet again, and the temperature rises suddenly and stays incredibly high till the climax of the novel. Heat waves do occur naturally, even in England, but Rushdie seems to be deliberately blurring the frontier between magic and realism, letting the one leak into the other, as Gibreel's dreams leak into his waking life.

A not dissimilar phenomenon, moreover, can be detected in the treatment of Saladin's metamorphosed state. Many things conspire to torment him during his stay at the Shaandaar Café, but what infuriates him most is the news the Gibreel will be starring in three new "theologicals" based on the life of Muhammad—the Gibreel who refused to recognize him at Rosa Diamond's, leaving him instead to the not-so-tender mercies of the police. In a development that goes unnoticed, the rage that this piece of news throws him into causes his horns, which have been growing steadily at the Shaandaar, to shrink at least three quarters of an inch. A similar but much more extreme shrinkage occurs when Hind discovers that her daughter Mishal and Hanif, a young lawyer whose office is in the Shaandaar, are lovers; Hind blames this liaison on the influence of the diabolic visitor and insists that Saladin leave immediately. Eight feet tall by now, breathing yellow and black smoke from left and right nostrils respectively, and fearsome in his rage, Saladin is purged in the ensuing few hours of his bloated, metamorphosed form and "restored to his old shape, mother-naked but of entirely human aspect and proportions, *humanized*—is there any option but to conclude?—by the fearsome concentration of his hate" (294) for Gibreel. It is not clear, however, whether Rushdie's message is that righteous, justified anger is therapeutic or that the conventional, outward symptoms of evil may manifest themselves irrespective of, or even in inverse proportion to, its real presence. Likewise, it is immaterial whether one or the other of those messages or the need to dispose credibly of Saladin's diabolic accoutrements and to let him resume his role in the story was in fact the deciding factor in the decision to include the episode. What is at issue is that magic (or in this case "antimagic") is given a quasipsychological rationale.

It seems that, either by being used symbolically or by being half integrated into—half accounted for by—the realistic aspects of the narrative, the fantastic is being used in a more cautious and calculated manner in this book than in Rushdie's earlier ones. Not that the fall with which the book opens, for instance, is less incredible than most such magic. Yet something of the gay abandon of the M.C.C. meeting held nightly in Saleem's skull or of the triple pregnancy that brought forth Omar Khayyam has been lost. No longer is the magic a spontaneous, visceral, thumb-to-nose response by the third world to the patriarchal rationality of the West, or even by Günter Grass to the unbelievably and unanswerably crass history of Europe through which he has had to live. The strategy at work in this most recent Rushdie novel is more deliberate, more manipulative. Breaking down the barriers between reality and fantasy, letting each "leak" into the other till the reader cannot dismiss the latter as mere fantasy—or the former, for that matter, as mere reality—becomes part of Rushdie's overall strategy. Metamorphosis alone is not enough. Taken together with human migration and cultural miscegenation, it must lead to less rigid categorization and demarcation, encourage more fluidity and inclusiveness, and thus create more flexibility and adaptability for the future.

Saladin's reentry into the mainstream of events enables the reader to see the significance of the concept of metamorphosis within the novel widen still further. Even before he emerges from hiding, a kind of awareness of his existence spreads through the immigrant population of London. And in parodic tribute to the liberatingly symbolic, revolutionary significance that accrued to the figure of Satan during and after the Romantic movement, Rushdie has Saladin invade the dreams of young West Indians, Indians, and Pakistanis, who begin to wear horned headbands as a symbol of resistance to police harassment. Whether as an illegal immigrant, a monarch in exile, a terrifying criminal, or a race hero, "Saladin Chamcha was getting to be true. . . . In his attic, slowly, Saladin Chamcha grew" (288). A curiosity worth noting, however, is that this symbol of rebellious, postcolonial opposition to continuing and oppressive paternalism directs all his hatred at a fellow colonial. Not for nothing does Rushdie have Saladin shorten his family name of *Chamchawala* to *Chamcha,* a word that in Urdu means both "spoon" and "sycophant."[3]

Things reach a climax, as does the novel, in a night of fire. Goaded by a vengeful Saladin—his many voices impersonate, telephonically and in satanically rhyming verses, Alleluia's many supposed lovers and regale Gibreel with accounts of her many assignations—Gibreel is once more a full-blown, full-time archangel. He roams the streets of London with a trumpet—a trumpet that lights fires in whatever direction it is pointed and played. Rioters help him in his mission by lighting their own fires. Saladin and Gibreel converge, unwittingly, so as to meet at the blazing Shaandaar Café. Chamcha plunges into the building in a futile attempt to rescue his former hosts; Gibreel, catching sight of his face and realizing in a flash the origin of all those voices on the telephone, nevertheless follows him in and drags him to safety, rescuing him from under a fallen beam. Later, Mishal Sufyan, accompanied by her lover and grieving for her dead parents, rides in the ambulance taking the two men to hospital. On the way she hears Gibreel, far into another dream, call out to another Mishal altogether: "Mishal! Come back! Nothing's happening! Mishal, for pity's sake; turn around, come back, come back" (469).

Briefly, then, and with ironic inappropriateness, Chamcha the Anglophile "toady" acts as a rallying symbol for immigrant resistance to white resentment at this invasion by Byron's "sun-burnt nations." More generally and more fittingly, the novel's obsessive emphasis on metamorphosis underlines the degree of change that immigrants must be prepared to undergo as well as the reciprocal changes that the immigrant's fresh way of viewing things can bring to the host society and that the society can benefit from if it is willing to accept them. Increasingly, as Gibreel's dreams and fantasies leak into his waking life, so the boundaries between fantasy and realism become blurred throughout the novel. Finally, the metamorphic extremes represented by Gibreel and Saladin in the guises of Archangel Gibreel/Gabriel and Archangel Emeritus Shaitan/Satan offer Rushdie an opportunity to comment on the nature of good and evil. Asked about the polarity between them in an interview, Rushdie replied (in terms it is hard to take at face value in view of his insistence elsewhere on breaking down the barriers implicit in other such dichotomies): "I had thought that the devil-angel relationship would be straightforward. What I found was that my view of them changed radically. And it was when I came to see how the emotional lives of these two characters connected that I began to know how to write the book. But it took ages."[4]

Of that relationship we do not see very much. They meet on the plane, Saladin clearly knowing all about Gibreel and Gibreel clearly knowing nothing about Saladin. Gibreel irritates Saladin from the start by his Indianness, his familiarity, and his self-absorbed tactlessness. He addresses Saladin as "Spoon," "Spoono" and "my old Chumch" (83) and drives Saladin "wild with anger and frustration" (85) at having to listen endlessly to accounts of his affair with Alleluia. All this irritation is as nothing, however, compared to the humiliation when he, Saladin Chamcha, British citizen par excellence, is arrested on suspicion of being an illegal immigrant if not worse, while Gibreel is not even questioned and pretends not to recognize him. They do not meet again for months, leaving plenty of time for Saladin's resentment against the man he sees as the author of all his woes to gather strength. When they do meet, at a party on a film studio's multiset recreation of Dickensian London, Saladin is alone—Pamela is with

Jumpy—while Gibreel is there with Alleluia and surrounded by many of the best-known guests. Perhaps there is enough here to make the revenge Saladin plans seem credible. What there is by no means enough of, however, is evidence either of Gibreel's angelic or Saladin's diabolic qualities. On balance, most readers are likely to see Saladin as more sinned against than sinning—though his final revenge is grotesquely excessive—and Gibreel, who drives both of the women who love him to suicide, as the reverse—though ultimately he suffers more. But this demonstrates little or nothing about the nature of good and evil, other than what would appear to be the resounding cliché that they overlap, interpenetrate, and can be mistaken for one another. One is reminded of the passage in *Shame* (265–67) in which Rushdie pontificates in a similarly uncharacteristic manner on the less than complete polarization of the populace into absolute Dantons and undiluted Robespierres.

Rushdie more or less admits as much when, anticlimactically, he defines the main differences between his twin protagonists as being those of "conjoined opposites," one continually blamed for crimes he has not committed and the other seen as angelically innocent of those he has, one as "somewhat less than life-size" and the other as congenitally larger than life. Most fundamentally and most relevantly as regards the major theme of the book, Gibreel, for all his instability and inconstancy, wishes to remain "joined to and arising from his past," whereas Saladin chooses to sever himself from his past, to begin again. By thus being in the one case "true" and in the other "false" to themselves, they can, "to follow the logic of our established terminology," be seen as good and evil respectively (426–27).

Apropos of Gibreel and Saladin as immigrants, this value judgment is a shrewd, interesting, and relevant observation that wisely steers clear of either challenging or endorsing the concepts of absolute good and evil. It might even be thought worthy of elevation to a generalization. In Saladin's case, moreover, the diagnosis is borne out by his insistence that he is "British" but that Mishal and Anahita are in no way entitled to feel the same way about themselves (258–59). The British trait he has most successfully adopted is that of snobbery, whether social or racial. To the extent, therefore, that exclusivity is a cardinal sin in Rushdie's eyes and acceptance or inclusiveness a cardinal virtue, Saladin deserves his horns. Gibreel, on the other hand, while remaining uncompromisingly Indian (and especially so in his vices), insists on being accepted—and accepted on exactly those terms—as at least any Englishman's equal. To that extent he deserves his halo. But are all the theological trappings that accompany such symbols either necessary or appropriate to the making of such a point? The reader is left with more than a suspicion that Rushdie's main purpose in having Gibreel and Saladin reincarnated as angel and devil respectively is to establish a stronger link between dream and reality by providing each narrative stream with an angelic and a diabolic presence.

A similar motivation may have prompted the somewhat anomalous half-dozen or so instances in which Satan steps forward and comments on what is happening—instances occurring as often in episodes of reality as in Gibreel's dreams. Rushdie seems to have decided against making more extensive and consistent use of the device—but more of that later.

The final example of metamorphosis occurs in the most moving and unexpected episode in the novel—its closing section. Rushdie more than once has said, of the Saladin in him who has chosen to live and work in England, that the process of being unprooted does not necessarily lead to rootlessness—that it can lead to a kind of multiple rooting.[5] Furthermore, even before the response to *The Satanic Verses* made any return to India impossible, it was clear that Rushdie would never go back on a permanent basis. Yet Saladin does. Moreover, though all three of Rushdie's previous novels end in disintegration, *The Satanic Verses* does not. At its end Saladin Chamcha bids fair to be reintegrated into Indian society and reinstated with his Indian lover as Salahuddin Chamchawala, having already become reconciled with his dying father. Protean to the last, Rushdie's fictional alter ego is finally made to embody the necessary if in most cases necessarily impossible dream that every migrant carries in his baggage, and to fetch his metamorphoses full circle till in their end is their beginning.

Gibreel's Dreams

Jahilia The first dream takes us to the desert city of Jahilia, "the whole of it a miracle worked by its citizens, who have learned the trick of transforming the fine white dune-sand of those forsaken parts,—the very stuff of inconstancy,—the quintessence of unsettlement, shifting, treachery, lack-of-form,—and have turned it, by alchemy, into the fabric of their newly invented permanence" (94). *Jahilia* merely means "ignorance," though it seems to be a term of almost universal disapproval most commonly used to refer to

the "period of ignorance" before the coming of Islam. Modern fundamentalists . . . designate the contemporary Muslim world as *jahiliya*: the word resonates not just with the idea of ignorance, but arrogance and impiety as well. In the theology of doubt, *jahili* is what fundamentalism is: ignorance combined with the arrogance of religious certainty. Jahilia is where Abraham, "the bastard," abandons his wife Hagar in the waterless wilderness. For the devout Muslim, this act of Abraham, the original *hanif* or monotheist, is a commendable instance of his absolute faith in God; for a modern sensibility, nurtured in a universe where ethics have broken free from the religious matrix, Abraham's act seems appallingly callous.[6]

From the outset we are in a world of controversy. Rushdie chooses a loaded word to designate the Mecca in which Muhammad is beginning his mission, just as he uses the medieval term *Mahound*—a much more abusive one than *Jahilia*—as Muhammad's name. Rushdie rationalizes the latter as his attempt to do what "Whigs, tories, and Blacks" did when they "chose to wear with pride the names they were given in scorn" (93). One may sympathize with him, faced by the problem of finding a name for Muhammad that will make him fictional yet leave him as recognizably historical. But for one man to hope to achieve the same kind of rehabilitation in a single novel that it took a whole community decades of living to do is too naive or too specious to be taken seriously. As if to add insult to injury, moreover, he clearly uses this city of sand[7] as a metaphor for the viability of doubt as a basis for human creativity and capacity to achieve. More importantly, we see in the range of possible responses to Abraham's abandoning Hagar in obedience to God a clear example of the diversity of viewpoint that has led to the whole controversy over *The Satanic Verses*.[8] However, that the differences between the value systems of different cultures and religions can be every inch as deep-seated and irreconcilable as those between the beliefs of supporters and opponents of abortion should come as no surprise to most observers of the human scene.

The dreamer is the actor Gibreel, and in the dream Gibreel is Archangel Gibreel, observing the action from a host of different camera angles (the movie talk is as pervasive as in *Midnight's Children*) and sometimes participating in it. Mahound requires him as a constant go-between in ascertaining Allah's wishes in these early days of Islam—which Rushdie tells us, provocatively, is the Arabic word for "submission." If we are to believe the Gibreel of the dream, however, Allah never enters into the picture. First Mahound climbs the mountain, and Gibreel, resentful of this continual demand for answers to questions but yielding to "his old weakness for taking too many roles" (108), prepares to play archangel and messenger. Mahound falls into a trancelike sleep and

feels a dragging pain in the gut, like something trying to be born, and now Gibreel, who has been hovering-above-looking-down, feels a confusion, *who am I,* in these moments it begins to seem that the archangel is actually *inside the Prophet,* I am the dragging in the gut, I am the archangel being extruded from the sleeper's navel, I emerge, Gibreel Farishta, while my other self, Mahound, lies *listening,* entranced, I am bound to him, navel to navel, by a shining cord of light, not possible to say which of us is dreaming the other. We flow in both directions along the umbilical cord. (110, author's emphasis)

On these occasions, Gibreel is often resentful toward a Supreme Being who is never available to provide the answers to Mahound's questions. Instead, awestruck by the force of personality emanating from the Prophet, Gibreel finds that this force is actually working his jaw and literally putting words into his mouth. Thus, when Mahound is first of all authorized to recognize the trinity of pre-Islamic goddesses and later informed that such authorization was the work of Shaitan impersonating Gibreel, the voice is the same on both occasions.

In defending himself against the charge of disrespect if not blasphemy, Rushdie emphasized that "this entire sequence happens in a dream, the fictional dream of a fictional character, an Indian movie star, and one who is losing his mind, at that."[9] Clearly, moreover, the style of speaking is that of Gibreel the twentieth-century actor. When asked in a radio interview how closely his treatment of Muhammad's life was based on historical fact, however, Rushdie replied: "Almost entirely."[10] He is in fact far too precisely on target in the passage discussed above to be in a position to deny that he has any such target. And that target is fundamentalism—the belief that there exists a single written source in which the divine mind has revealed to human minds (in the case of Islam, to a single human mind) the total truth, frozen for all time, concerning that divine mind's nature and purposes. In other words, fundamentalism is the belief that there have existed, in time, human minds capable of understanding the entire and unalterable nature and purposes of the divine mind for all time. Or, to reverse the proposition, fundamentalism implies that the divine mind is of such limited nature and entertains purposes that are so limited in scope as to be communicable to and comprehensible by, in their entirety and for all time, one or more human minds. That last proposition, to my all-too-human mind, seems the ultimate blasphemy. Furthermore, no other religion makes such a claim as specifically as does Islam. In its extreme form, Islam states that the Qur'an is uncreated and has always existed in its untranslatable Arabic form as part of the divine mind.[11] Understandably, therefore, the fact that Rushdie exploited, used as the very title of the book, and brought to the world's notice a legend such as that of the satanic verses is a source of distress and anger to fundamentalist Muslims. To many the mere possibility of Muhammad's having been misled by Shaitan in even one detail opens up horrifying possibilities.

In reality the Qur'an existed for some time in fragmentary disorder and was not assembled into its present form and "canonized" until some time after Muhammad's death[12]—in other words, it was in part the work of ordinary human labors and human judgment and therefore subject to a human capacity for error, just like any other holy book. Moreover, "the legal doctrine of 'abrogation,' according to which some Qur'anic verses are deemed to be superseded by others as sources of law," and which as already noted the satanic verses have been seen as justifying,[13] clearly implies the need for the continued use of human judgment to interpret and apply divinely revealed truth. Much more fundamentally, however, what Rushdie is implying in the extracts above is that the play of human judgment and capacity for human error is intrinsic to the process of revelation itself. He who claims to have a "hot line" to the deity may be hearing what he wants to hear or all unwittingly listening to his own prerecorded messages. It is on this issue that Islam and Rushdie part company most decisively. Rushdie is above all the child of an age of doubt—an age when "honest doubt" is no longer merely the prerequisite of "honest faith" but has become the one thing left in which to place one's faith. What Milan Kundera refers to as "the wisdom of uncertainty"[14] has become a positive rather than a negative quality—the only form of truth it is safe to believe in, since it acknowledges the provisional and subjective elements in all discovery and all knowledge. All of which is anathema to fundamentalists of any kind, since it involves building on sand rather than rock—or building *with* sand.

Ironically there has been far less indignation expressed about the passage above, which injects a subjective element into the whole process of revelation, than about the one describing how insertions and changes are deliberately made by the scribe, Salman, when writing the inspired words dictated by Gibreel and repeated by Mahound.[15] The former, while not denying the possibility of revelation, raises the specter of all revealed truth's being subject to close inspection and verification, whereas the latter merely demonstrates how a word here or a word there can be changed and no one be the wiser. In itself it is highly "revealing" that revealed truths can be felt to inhere in every word of the form in which they have come down to us and to be more threatened by a slight change in that outward form than by their entire basis being called into question.

Even more revealing, though not surprising, is the indignation aroused by what are felt to be the disrespectful or flippantly colloquial terms

Rushdie uses, or has his characters use, when referring to Mahound and his disciples. Yet surely the comment "and some sort of bum from Persia by the outlandish name of Salman" (101) is a piece of mock self-deprecation. "That bunch of riff-raff" and "those *goons*—those fucking *clowns*" (author's emphasis) are phrases used by characters hostile to Mahound, and "this trinity of scum" (101) is said by a narrator ironically using the same linguistic register as the company on whom he is eavesdropping. But quite apart from the fact that most such critics of *The Satanic Verses* have not read the novel, it is unlikely even if they had that they would make distinctions of this order. For though poetry has a long and distinguished history in Arabic, fiction—and certainly anything resembling twentieth-century fiction in English—is a very new arrival in the Muslim world. Along with representation in the visual arts, such secondary, imitative creation is still regarded by some as a tautological affront to the original creator. So, not surprisingly, the conventions of fiction are unfamiliar to most Muslims, and those of postmodernist fiction even more so.

Finally, there is the matter of Mahound's wives. After his first wife, the wealthy widow who sets her much younger second husband up in business, dies, he permits his followers to take four wives each and acquires a round dozen himself, in some cases at least for political reasons. Their historical equivalents, since chosen by the Prophet himself, are regarded with great veneration by Muslims. The wives themselves scarcely put in an appearance in the novel. But much of the section entitled "Return to Jahilia" is set in a brothel known as "The Curtain," which, when Mahound first returns in triumph to the city he was forced to flee, is spared as part of his plan to wean the inhabitants gently from their less puritanical habits. (Prayers five times a day, no alcohol, and the locking up of wives are deemed enough to start with.) When the twelve resident whores decide to adopt the names and as far as possible the personalities of Mahound's twelve wives, the idea is a great commercial success. The suggestion comes in the first place from Baal, a satiric poet hired in the bad old days to lampoon Mahound and his followers and now a refugee in The Curtain. Eventually, at their request, he marries all twelve ministrants, thus rendering unequivocal his role of anti-Mahound "in that anti-mosque, that labyrinth of profanity" (383).

The writing in this section is vintage Rushdie—comic, inventive, uninhibitedly irreverent, even tender. It is all the more offensive for that, of course, to those who take offense. In fact, it is to this episode more often than any other that angry letters to the press have referred. Nor does it affect the issue that many mistakenly accuse Rushdie of saying that Muhammad's wives themselves rather than their parodic equivalents were prostitutes; the offense might be greater in the latter case, since the insult would seem meaninglessly gratuitous. Nor would it help matters if the writers could begin to understand the nature and role of parody, since Rushdie's intention here would seem to be to emphasize the servile role that Islam, as a function of being part of the culture of its time and place as well as of bringing about change within that culture, imposed on women. What more servile female role than that of prostitute? What an insult to Islamic marriage!

Yet in fact, so far from stressing the degrading or repellant aspects of life behind The Curtain, Rushdie uses a tone that blends comedy and sentimentality. There is pathos but no parodic irony in his account of these whores' "fantasy of 'ordinary life' in which they wanted nothing more than to be obedient, and—yes—submissive helpmeets of a man who was wise, loving and strong." The situation appears to be made all the more innocuous, moreover, when the headship of this tenderly unholy household is assumed by the aging and perforce gentle Baal, who begins to write again, the poetry that comes to him being "the sweetest he had ever written" (384).

This polarity between Mahound and Baal, prophet and satirist, has been clear from the outset and is made quintessentially so when the latter, sentenced to die with his "wives," goes to that death saying, "Whores and writers, Mahound. We are the people you can't forgive." Mahound replies, "Writers and whores. I see no difference here" (392). It is also clear that Rushdie identifies with Baal, the skeptical, irreverent spokesperson for a city built on and out of sand, more closely than with anyone else in the dream. So in contrast to Rushdie's self-proclaimed feminism in *Shame*, The Curtain must be seen as a parody that presents a desirable alternative to Mahound's household rather than a travesty of it—even a permissive, loving alternative. Once one has allowed oneself to think of a brothel in such terms, moreover, the House of the Rising Sun in *Grimus* must come to mind. Like The Curtain, it acts as a kind of refuge—even, as Rushdie indicates, a sanctuary such that the most aggressive citizens of K would not dream of "violating the sanctity o' the House" (*Grimus*, 236–67). Furthermore, the concern for others and the sensitivity to their feelings that its ministrants show, together with their sense of guardianship over the community's few remaining saving graces, confirm that Rushdie did indeed intend to create a "blasphemous" parody of more conventionally religious "houses."

I hesitate to claim that there are adequately close parallels in the intervening novels to warrant an overall brothel-based reading of Rushdie's work. Remembering, however, that The Curtain is a "labyrinth" of love, one might recall that in *Midnight's Children,* at the heart of the "incomprehensibly labyrinthine salt-water channels overtowered by the cathedral-arching trees" (*M.C.* 349) of the Ganges Delta as it flows through the Sundarbans, Saleem Sinai and his three fellow soldiers come across the Hindu temple bedizened in erotica where, night after night, they make love to four identical beauties (355). Finally, though the labyrinth that begins and ends *Shame* is no brothel, it is a strongly matriarchal labyrinth framing a novel that also includes the "archmatriarch" Bariamma. And the mixed dormitory over which she presides after dark is quite sufficiently labyrinthine, Rani conjectures, to offer some of the opportunities a brothel does.

Tradition has it, however ironically, that brothels are matriarchal by definition, and this assessment is certainly true of Rushdie's. Even in the Hindu temple the solace offered Saleem and his fellow warriors is presided over by the statue of Kali—as formidable a madam as one can imagine. Rushdie leaves the reader little option but to see bordellos as, by definition, fortresses of a femininity calculated to arouse nostalgia in any male breast, offering solace, nurture, refuge from a harsh world outside, and women who "in their heart of hearts . . . wished to turn themselves into the oldest male fantasy of all" (*S.V.,* 384). Moreover, the negative ingredients of this elixir of womanliness are equally stereotypical: Jocasta's attempt to protect Virgil from doing what it is his duty and destiny to do (*Grimus* 167–68, 243); the leakage of "virtue" that can unman football players the night before a match and that makes Saleem and companions "translucent as glass" (*M.C.,* 356); the overprotectiveness of Omar Khayyam's three mothers; the whole labyrinthine quality of a man's relationship with any woman. It is tempting to try to see the episode as parody of a highly ironic kind—a modest proposal for putting male-female relationships on a sound footing. But how are we then to read the final "highnoon" showdown between Baal and Muhammad? Can we deny the former his moment of victory in defeat, or the latter, who spares the lives of Salman and even Hind, his moment of intolerance? Small wonder some women critics are skeptical about Rushdie's championing of their cause.

To return, therefore, to the response of a Muslim readership to this portion of *The Satanic Verses* is to perceive a doubly poignant irony in the fact that this is the part of the novel that gives them greatest offense. It offends many non-Muslims too, though mainly as a gratuitous and less than wholly relevant digression in dubious taste. As Malise Ruthven argues with reference to the whole novel, however: "The focus for the outrage . . . is less the raising of doubt than the lampooning of the Prophet." And the section of the novel in which such lampooning is perceived to take place most outrageously is the brothel sequence. That much is clear, but Ruthven continues revealingly:

Many Christians, of course, have been similarly offended by the appearance of Christ in profane situations—notably in the recent row over Martin Scorsese's film of Kazantzakis's novel *The Last Temptation,* where Jesus fantasises about sexual relations with Mary Magdalene. To note the parallels, however, is also to become aware of the differences. If *Imitatio Muhammadi,* as Armand Abel has astutely observed, is an imitation of the Prophet's activity, *Imitatio Christi* is rather the imitation of Christ's suffering. . . . To insult Christ is only to offend those Christians who have so lost touch with the Christian *weltanschauung* that they forget that true Christians expect to be insulted, just as Jesus himself was reviled and tormented to death. . . . The Christian response to insult is to try to gain the moral and psychological advantage, to "turn the other cheek."

The Islamic model is diametrically different. The Prophet did not urge his followers to love their enemies or to turn the other cheek.[16]

Reading elsewhere in Ruthven's book of the Muslim sense of *izzat* or "honor," of how much this is bound up with the defense of a man's womenfolk, and of the collective and vulnerable izzat of minority Muslim communities in, say, the north of England, which any insult to the Prophet and above all the Prophet's wives can so mortally offend, I remembered an authorial intrusion in *Shame.* It tells of a Muslim father living in London who is driven to kill his daughter "because by making love to a white boy she had brought such dishonour upon her family that only her blood could wash away the stain" (123). Comparing two such causes of offense and in neither case being able to empathize with the response but in one having no option but to believe in its horrifying sincerity, I came closer to understanding the burning of *The Satanic Verses* in Bradford, that phlegmatic north of England city where, long before the Pakistanis came, I was a boy. And I wondered whether Rushdie had ever compared the two cases.

Ayesha and Ayesha   Mahound's youngest wife is named Ayesha (as was Muhammad's), and she is mentioned in a conversation between Salman and Baal (386–87). There must be and is, therefore, a young prostitute who has assumed the name (379–80). But two further Ayeshas play leading roles in the remaining dreams—the two twentieth-century dreams—in which Gibreel is archangel. Although this is the only instance where Rushdie goes so far as to use the same name four times over, his penchant for repeating names is as ubiquitous and as mechanically functional rather than symbolically significant as what he calls his leitmotivs in *Midnight's Children,* "recurring things in the plot, incidents or objects or phrases which in themselves have no meaning or no particular meaning but which form a kind of non-rational network of connections in the book. . . . a sheet with a hole in it . . . a silver spittoon . . . a game of snakes and ladders . . . a hand with a pointing finger. . . ."[17] Alleluia's last name, for instance, is Cone (a mutation of Cohen), and the mountain Mahound climbs to seek answers from Gibreel is inevitably named Mount Cone. The wives of Abu Simbel, ruler of Jahilia, and Muhammad Sufyan, proprietor of the Shaandaar Café, besides both being much stronger personalities than their husbands, are both called Hind. Hind Sufyan's elder daughter shares the name Mishal with Mishal Akhtar, a pivotal figure in the second of the forthcoming dreams. In all three cases one character (or mountain) appears in the special dream sequences and the other in the regular story line—a factor that makes an obtrusive if minor contribution to helping hold together a novel that threatens even more than *Midnight's Children* to fly apart at the seams. The most eerily telling link is that between the two Mishals, who practically meet one another when Gibreel is watched by one in the back of an ambulance as he speaks to the other in his dream.

All four of the Ayeshas, however, exist in Gibreel's dreams. The consequent dubiety of their status alone might give us pause. It is easy enough to accept, compassionately, the notion that people from Nigeria or Senegal can be "described" into growing tails or becoming more than 50 percent water buffalo. But that all of us are mostly made up of mental concepts is much harder to accept: that we are like Gibreel, trapped in the fiercely importunate needs of Rosa Diamond or Mahound; like Pamela, trapped in Saladin's need to be English and, like Saladin, trapped in Pamela's need to escape being English; like the twelve whores, who assume the names of Mahound's twelve wives and find the desires and expectations of their customers confirm them in their new identities till they even forget their old names—that is, that all of us are shaped by the idea and the expectations others have of us and the idea and expectations we come to have of ourselves. This ability/liability to think or dream ourselves (or to be thought or dreamed by others) into new forms is emphasized over and over in Gibreel's first dream. *"What kind of idea are you? Man-or-mouse?"* whispers a voice in Mahound's ear (95). *"What kind of idea am I?"* Abu Simbel asks himself (102). "Should God be proud or humble, majestic or simple, yielding or un-? *What kind of idea is he? What kind am I?"* asks Mahound (111). "I want the fight. To the death; that is the kind of idea I am. What kind are you?" asks Hind of Mahound (121). Finally, in one of his archangelic phases in London, a confused Gibreel overhears the slurred voice of Baal saying: *"Any new idea, Mahound, is asked two questions. The first is asked when it's weak: WHAT KIND OF IDEA ARE YOU? Are you the kind that compromises, does deals, accomodates itself to society, aims to find a niche, to survive; or are you the cussed, bloody-minded, ramrod-backed type of damnfool notion that would rather break than sway with the breeze?—The kind that will almost certainly, ninety-nine times out of a hundred, be smashed to bits; but, the hundredth time, will change the world"* (335, author's emphasis).[18]

Lest this final quotation should seem to gainsay all that the others implied about the potential for change, however, Baal in person, in the second half of the Jahilia dream, addresses an absent Mahound, about to return to Jahilia, thus: "And now, Mahound, on your return to Jahilia, time for the second question: How do you behave when you win? When your enemies are at your mercy and your power has become absolute: what then?" (369). Whereupon Mahound shows, by his clemency to almost all such enemies, that he is flexible once he is sure of his strength.

To return to Gibreel's later, twentieth-century dreams, however, the first of these begins with a brilliant description of an Imam in exile in London, scheming a glorious return to a homeland rather like the Ayatollah Khomeini's, except that Empress Ayesha sits on the throne. Even more chilling than the account of the physical siege maintained against a hostile world is that of the need he feels to defend his belief from the constant threat of ideas—the hatred of all change, of all potential for metamorphosis. For the revolution the Imam longs for will not just overthrow the tyrant Ayesha but also defeat "History" herself—History and all her hateful progeny, "progress, science, rights," History that is mere delusion, since all necessary knowledge has been revealed by Al-Lah to Mahound (210).

Such a portrait, had it been brought to the Ayatollah's notice, would surely have earned Rushdie a second death sentence. Far more dangerously reprehensible than mere disrespect for Khomeini, moreover, is the shrewd, clear-sighted analysis of the irreconcilable differences that separate Rushdie and the fundamentalists.

What follow are scenes of grotesque comedy and horrific symbolism, as the Imam leaps on to Gibreel's shoulders and demands to be flown to the empress's palace, where, he promises, "I will show you love." What we in fact witness is the household guards mowing down the advancing crowd of people with "giggling" machine guns, and as "the hill of the dead grows higher" (213) the people must clamber over it in order to continue advancing ("You see how they love me," says the Imam) until finally they reach the soldiers and the guns are silenced. At this point the dome of the palace bursts open and the figure of Al-Lat, one of the three goddesses Mahound almost allowed to share power with Al-Lah, rises from it, "glowing with blackness" (214). Gibreel is ordered to kill her and, just as happened with

Mahound, he has no choice—"he is a marionette going to war," obedient to a stronger will than his own. When finally, like a comic-book hero, he destroys her with thunderbolts supplied by the Imam, the last image he sees before the dream ends is "the Imam grown monstrous, lying in the palace forecourt with his mouth yawning open at the gates; as the people march through the gates he swallows them whole" (215).

The echoes of the earlier dream are clearly intended to show that, whether knowing what they do or not, human beings have always manipulated the supernatural beings they create in their own image. Gibreel is as powerless to resist the Imam's wishes as he was to resist Mahound's. But there is a danger, surely, in Rushdie's implying too close a resemblance between Mahound and the Imam. Such a likeness is implied while the Imam is still in London, since three of his young followers—Khalid, Salman, and Bilal—bear the same names as three of Mahound's (and the historical Muhammad's) disciples. It is confirmed, moreover, when we are told that behind the empress's palace rises "a mountain of almost perfectly conical dimensions" (213). Rushdie has elsewhere expressed profound respect for Muhammad as a religious pioneer, in contrast to his disrespect for those who claim, directly on behalf of the Prophet and indirectly on their own behalf as his interpreters, an infallibility and a quasidivine status to which Muhammad himself laid no claim.[19] Why then, if Rushdie wishes us to believe him, should he thus seem to imply that the Imam in his novel is Muhammad all over again, neither better nor worse? The use of repeated names, visual details, and images (even identical heights for Mount Everest and the exploding plane) can become a fetish.

The final dream, like the one set in Jahilia, is a two-part serial, the first half following immediately on the dream about the Imam without a chapter break. This setup makes the reader more vulnerable to the apparent tone of the story at its outset—less suspicious of irony and more willing to believe that God "can be a God of love, as well as one of vengeance, power, duty, rules and hate" (216). The story is the very simple one of Ayesha, a girl wearing and eating nothing but butterflies, who persuades a whole village that the Archangel Gabriel has appeared to her in a number of visions and given her a number of messages. Finally there is a command that everyone in the village (a Moslem one) go on a pilgrimage on foot to Mecca. The fact that the village is in India and that the Arabian sea lies between them and their destination does not disconcert Ayesha in the least. The waters will part for them. "Everything is required of us, and everything will be given" (235) is her answer to any problem that arises.

The Mishal of the story is wife of the very wealthy local landowner, Mirza

Saeed Akhtar. Ayesha tells her she has an advanced, incurable cancer, the very idea of which her husband ridicules, but specialists in the nearest city confirm the diagnosis. The only hope is the pilgrimage. So she and her mother, a banker's wife from the city, join the villagers and set out for the sea, 200 miles away, with Mirza Saeed bringing up the rear in his air-conditioned Mercedes-Benz, still trying to dissuade his wife from all this folly.

Everything goes wrong on the journey, yet everything also goes right; they reach the coast, stand on the shore, and the butterflies, which have followed them all the way, create the shape of a gigantic angel in the sky. Watched by Mirza Saeed, whose final attempt to stop his wife fails and who is left calling after her, "Come back. Nothing is happening; come back" (502), they wade out into the water. Then, at a certain distance from the shore, without a sign of a struggle, the waders' heads disappear under the water. Only a few stragglers are rescued or turn back; the drowned bodies of most of the rest wash ashore in time. Yet all but one of the survivors agree, totally independently while under police interrogation with a view to possible prosecution for attempted illegal emigration, that they saw the waters part and those ahead of them walking on the sea bed.

Many details have been changed, but the story is based on an actual incident that even ended with the survivors being prosecuted for illegal emigration, though the pilgrimage in that case was to have been to Kerbala in Iraq.[20] Sometimes fantasy is overtaken by reality in the race toward absurdity.

In this dream Gabriel is just as helplessly under the control of a village girl as he was under that of Mahound or the Imam. Indeed, since he has no memory of what happens after being summoned to her side and falling into a deep trance—no recollection of relaying messages to her, of diagnosing cancer for her, or of flying with her "into the highest heights . . . even to the lote-tree of the uttermost end" (235)—he feels more helplessly manipulated than ever. Not infrequently does innocence have just such a ruthless unanswerability when acting under inspiration. Nor is the deity from whom her messages emanate by any means self-evidently "a God of love." It is even arguable that the villagers are just as taken in and exploited by her delusions as are the people the Imam "liberates" from the Empress Ayesha; certainly a higher percentage die in the process. Cheered by Rushdie's assurance of a story about a "God of love," we are then ambushed by retrospective irony as these unloving consequences of the latest set of divine pronouncements wrung from Gibreel unfold.

Nevertheless, there is clearly a difference between the Imam and

Ayesha. However enigmatically, the very fact that she shares a name with his archenemy may imply as much. Her exploitation of Gibreel has dire results that are not of a wholly different order to the normal outcome of drought, famine, flood, or disease in an Indian village. Her condoning of a foundling baby's being stoned to death, though it stuns her simple followers into mutinous immobility, is hardly comparable to the Imam's drooling over the "love" shown him by the thousands marching to their death. It is even arguable that Ayesha brought a purpose and a meaning to those simple villagers' lives and that they died happy, though deludedly so. Mirza Saeed himself, reason and Rushdie's representative in the story one would have thought, is a broken man at the end. Nor is this merely because of his wife's death. The final straw is to discover that, despite having rushed into the sea at the last minute to where she disappeared, he is the only survivor not to have seen the waters part and the pilgrims walking on the sea floor. Not until he is dying of sheer grief-induced inanition does he finally see the waters part. In this story Rushdie is clearly saying that unbelievers as well as believers would do well to acknowledge "the wisdom of uncertainty."

Equally clearly, however, Rushdie is implying that the religious experience is always fraught with the potential for self-deception and the subsequent deception of others. This can be seen even at the humble and apparently innocent village level, in a simple child of nature arrayed, as not even Solomon in all his glory was, in butterflies. For surely, in the unnecessarily prolonged way in which Ayesha shows Mirza Saeed how each butterfly her fingers flick back into her mouth remains "fluttering within the dark cavern of its death, . . . making no attempt to escape" (219), we are shown the equal power that she will come to exercise over the villagers.

One final detail distinctly indicates that Rushdie intends Ayesha's mission to be analogous to Mahound's. On their last night together, when the villagers are seriously and mutinously discussing returning home, Mirza Saeed offers to fly Ayesha, Mishal, and a dozen villagers direct to Mecca. The offer is couched in flattering terms, and Ayesha is seriously tempted. But after consulting Gibreel she remains faithful to her original vision, and the narrator comments: "His offer had contained an old question: *What kind of idea are you?* And she, in turn, has offered him an old answer. *I was tempted, but am renewed; am uncompromising; absolute; pure*" (500, author's emphasis). She too rejects the satanic revision—the more palatable compromise—and holds stubbornly to her original idea. Hers is "smashed to bits," of course, but Mahound's "will change the world."

Narrative Voice and Style

In his first novel, *Grimus,* Rushdie's narrative voice used for the most part a conventional third-person point of view, with occasional first-person interventions by two or three characters. In *Midnight's Children* he wrote a first draft in the third person and revised it to a first-person form. Because in a prior incarnation it had existed in the third person, however, the story inherited a karma that it was not able to escape. Acres of manuscript covering multitudes of events Saleem could not possibly have witnessed and was unlikely to have been told about, including of course the 24 percent of the book that took place before he was even born, had already been written. When he first began the revision, however, Rushdie intended to use the first-person form in merely the prenatal portion of the narrative.[21] So, clearly, the kind of credibility that depends on realism was not his first priority. In this aspect of the book, as in so many others, Rushdie seems to be daring us to disbelieve the incredible. There is also a great deal of metafictional recapitulation, foreshadowing, and other commentary, all of it emphasizing—as if it were not obvious enough—the fictive nature of this particular piece of fiction. Much the same is true of *Shame.* Moreover, though the narrative of the latter is from a third-person point of view, much of the authorial commentary is unashamedly in the first person, buttonholing the reader almost as a nineteenth-century author might.

Narrative point of view in *The Satanic Verses* is also in the third person, as is authorial commentary (pages 426–27, for example), though the latter is much less in evidence than in *Shame.* In general, moreover, fewer liberties are taken with the normal conventions of prose in *The Satanic Verses* than in either *Midnight's Children* or *Shame.* There is, however, an unacknowledged and interesting shift into and out of first-person interior monologue in this account of just how Mahound receives his divinely inspired messages via Gibreel[22]:

. . . and now the miracle starts in his my our guts, he is straining with all his might at something, forcing something, and Gibreel begins to feel that force, here it is *at my own jaw* working it open, opening, shutting; and the power, starting within Mahound, reaching up to *my vocal cords* and the voice comes.

Mahound's eyes open wide, he's seeing some kind of vision, staring at it, oh, that's right, Gibreel remembers, me. He's seeing me. My lips moving, being moved by. What, whom? Don't know, can't say. Nevertheless, here they are, coming out of my mouth, up my throat, past my teeth: the Words. (112, author's emphasis)

Only during this encounter and the later one, when Mahound and Gibreel wrestle and their identities once again intermingle (122–23), is syntax thus wrenched back and forth between first and third person. Not even when Gibreel is drawn into Rosa Diamond's fluidly recreated memories of life and love in the Argentine, or when his dreams leak into his waking life and he shuttles back and forth abruptly between his human and angelic identities, do Rushdie's sentences fail to acknowledge the shifts to and fro between a direct and a reported stream of consciousness. Thus, through his syntax, Rushdie indicates the unique significance of these scenes between Gibreel and Mahound and of the metamorphic processes there recorded.

Of less importance but curious interest are narrational comments such as the following on the initial fall: "What did they expect? . . . Higher Powers had taken an interest . . . and such Powers (I am, of course, speaking of myself) have a mischievous, almost wanton attitude to tumbling flies.[23] And another thing, let's be clear: great falls change people. You think *they* fell a long way? In the matter of tumbles, I yield pride of place to no personage. . . ." (133). Clearly this is Shaitan, the fallen archangel, speaking. And he does so in at least five other places. On page 10, after claiming to have watched the whole fall of Gibreel and Saladin and asking: "Of what type— angelic, satanic—was Farishta's song? Who am I?" the voice continues: "Let's put it this way: who has the best tunes?"[24] On pages 92–93, having explained how humans are much more stubbornly persistent as doubters than most angels, he adds: "I know; devil talk. Shaitan interrupting Gibreel. Me?" On page 95, having referred to Ibrahim (Abraham) as a "bastard" for abandoning Hagar and their child in the waterless desert and saying God told him to, he adds: "From the beginning men used God to justify the unjustifiable. . . . Small wonder, then, that women have turned to me.—But I'll keep to the point; Hagar wasn't a witch" (i.e., wasn't one of those who turned to him). On pages 408–409, after declining to settle Chamcha's doubts about demonic influence and claiming to have resisted similar temptations to interfere in the action, he admits to having impersonated God and hastened Gibreel's departure from Alleluia's apartment. On page 457 he again refuses to interfere and influence Gibreel's choice as to whether to be the agent of God's wrath or of His love—to blow or not to blow his trumpet.

Interestingly, in the case of the comment on Ibrahim and Hagar, Malise Ruthven assumes the aside about men using God to justify the unjustifiable to be by "Rushdie/Gibreel."[25] More strikingly, moreover, in the case of the narrator's admitting to having impersonated God, Ruthven, Gayatri Spivak (whom Ruthven cites), and D. J. Enright (admittedly on the strength of a reviewer's hasty first reading) all assume the comments to be by the author.[26] Anything is possible in a Rushdie novel, of course. But were he to have created such a walk-on speaking part for the author and allowed him to communicate with other characters as well as with the reader, as Mozart improvised cadenzas to his own concertos, Rushdie would surely have used such a radical innovation much more extensively and in more fruitful ways than is the case in *The Satanic Verses*.

I take these oversights by otherwise perceptive readers to support, at least indirectly, my contention that there is no case to be made for Satan as the consistent narrator throughout the novel. There are in fact too many places where Rushdie is clearly (though much less obtrusively than in *Shame*) hawking his own views on the course of events. There are a number of places where, within his own dreams, Gibreel seems to be doing the narration. For the greater part of the book, where the narrator is unidentifiable, the tone of the writing neither is nor readily could become either recognizably or appropriately satanic. At a first reading, indeed, the instances cited above seem to be vestiges of an apparently promising but short-lived bright idea. And that in fact may be the explanation.

Yet the fluid, metamorphic nature of the whole novel suggests other possibilities. Sentences slide back and forth from third- to first- to third-person verbs and pronouns; the time frame switches from the twentieth to the seventh and back to the twentieth century, with twentieth-century idiom and thought patterns spoken by seventh-century minds and mouths and seventh-century thought patterns persisting in a twentieth-century imam; Saladin, in middescent to earth, feels himself "becoming metamorphic, hybrid, as if he were growing into the person whose head nestled now between his legs and whose legs were wrapped around his long, patrician neck" (7); Gibreel's mind, when dreaming, is invaded by Mahound's, or the Imam's, or Ayesha's, and when awake by Rosa Diamond's, each time any of them seeks answers or responses to their questions or desires; Gibreel acts in theologicals when awake and dreams theologicals when asleep, the latter state increasingly leaking into the former; Saladin, the more-English-than-the-English turncoat, unwittingly invades people's dreams in his diabolic form and becomes the reluctant symbol of mounting immigrant hostility to the English; the very notion of good and evil in any unequivocal sense is undermined if not invalidated as Gibreel and Saladin assume the outward form of archangel and devil but refuse to match their subsequent behavior to the expectations aroused by such metamorphoses; and so on and so forth, with fact and fiction, fantasy and realism continually and interchangeably shifting and switching like faces on a dance floor under strobe lighting. If, in fact, everything is subject to change and it becomes problematic where realism ends and fantasy begins and vice versa—if, in effect, something like the full implications of a post-Einsteinian relativistic universe are to be given formal fictive expression—should we be surprised that the narration, too, changes its points of view and tone of voice? If Saladin Chamcha qua horned beast can invade the dreams of immigrant youth, why shouldn't the original, of which Saladin is a mere parody, invade Gibreel's dreams? If as near the full truth as possible about this fantastic, variegatedly variable world is to be told, shouldn't the devil be allowed to have his say? The device is less than perfectly worked out and executed, and it is too infrequently used to establish a clear function for itself. But it offers at least a kind of challenge to authorial hegemony and serves to remind the reader that the opposition may have good ideas as well as good tunes.[27]

That much said, it should be admitted that there are no narrational tours de force like the pages climaxing in the birth of Saleem, Shiva, and Indian independence or the cinematic cutting back and forth between Ahmed and Amina Sinai as the former tries to leave his protection money, only to have it scattered by monkeys, while the latter fights her way with Lifafa Das between the clutching hands and stumps of Delhi's beggars to where she will have Saleem's enigmatic future enigmatically foretold. What we have in *The Satanic Verses,* in fact, is for the most part a fairly straightforward piece of third-person narration. The novel is almost completely devoid of foreshadowings, and the only metafictional technique used to remind us that this is fiction is that of interlarding the ongoing story with a series of dreams, which may or may not be seen as a new addition to the postmodernist arsenal. Nor are there any of the contrived recapitulations that besprinkle *Midnight's Children;* instead, there are polite biographical introductions of varying length to most of the characters, whether Gibreel Farishta, Saladin Chamcha, Pamela Chamcha, Alleluia Cone, Rosa Diamond, Muhammad and Hind Sufyan, Zeenat Vakil, Mimi Mamoulian, Hal Valance, or even Orphia Phillips. Reading a Rushdie novel is still some distance from reading Conrad's *Nostromo,* with its pages and pages of background as each major figure makes a first appearance, but it is closer than I had believed possible.

The overall style, too, is of a piece with the narrative strategies. There is still a marvelously flexible dexterity to the way Rushdie handles language. The passages quoted above, where sentences oscillate between first and third person, show him developing and refining a new technique for a new set of circumstances. In addition, in writing about London Rushdie has expanded his repertoire of voices and has shown himself able to capture the idiom of its teenagers shrewdly (245, 257–58), that of West Indian immigrants more dubiously (328–31), and that of dub or rap poetry (292) with the slick skills of a copywriter for television commercials. But the energy, the impulsive enthusiasm, the sentences that go on for anything from a page and a half to four pages, the sheer intoxication with language—all that is less exuberantly in evidence.

What is very much in evidence—and what is perhaps so breathtakingly risky that it demands a measure of control elsewhere—is the layered, double-club-sandwich, how-do-I-get-my-teeth-into-this-one structure of a five-hundred-page novel that is alternatingly half dream and half reality, the reality being impregnated with dreams and the dreams being full of political and religious reality; a novel with two heroes and half a dozen major themes even by its author's conscious count; a novel that could really fall apart, no matter how brilliant the pieces.

Social Satire

In acknowledging that "the metafictional strategies of *The Satanic Verses* are not nearly so pronounced" as those of *Midnight's Children* and *Shame,* Timothy Brennan argues that this difference is because "Rushdie is dealing with a life not only remembered and longed for but experienced first hand" and that "the characters are for the first time people living in the world, acting out their own lives in a story of their own" rather than in one where "the plotting of the characters was essentially an orchestration of parodic vignettes that collectively made up an argument." The implied comment on "metafictional strategies" aside, Brennan here puts his finger on an important new factor that went into the creation of *The Satanic Verses:* "England is where Rushdie lives (not India or Pakistan)."[28]

As already noted, one has only to look at the titles of some of Rushdie's nonfiction prose pieces about Margaret Thatcher's England to have some idea of his political interests and orientation. Although his journalism has also included such articles on the Indian subcontinent as "Truth Retreats When the Saint Goes Marching In: *Gandhi*" and "After Indira, an Awakening or the Whirlwind?",[29] their appearance in that organ of the establishment, *The Times,* rather than the more liberal or left-wing *Guardian* and *New Society,* suggests a lower degree of emotional commitment. Indeed, his most heartfelt polemics on the subject of India are to be found in "Outside the Whale" and "The Raj Revival"—articles chiefly concerned not with Indian or Pakistani politics but with an unhealthy British nostalgia for the days of the Raj and Britain's imperial heyday.[30]

So it is not surprising that in *The Satanic Verses,* the first novel to be set in the country in which it was written, the targets of his satire should at last be British. The scenes that, like afterimages on the retina, everyone remembers long after closing the book are those of the night of fire when Gibreel is wandering the streets, blowing "little fire-flowers out of his horn" that climb "like creepers up the sides of the towers" (462). Most haunting is his encounter, "behind the cathedrals of the Industrial Revolution, the railway termini of north London" (459), with the thirteen-, fourteen-, fifteen-year-old prey of johns and pimps alike.

They are moving towards him now, drawn to him like fishes on unseen hooks. As they near him their walks change, their hips lose their swagger, their faces start looking their age, in spite of all the make-up. When they reach him, they kneel. *Who do you say that I am?* he asks, and wants to add: *I know your names. I met you once before, elsewhere, behind a curtain. Twelve of you then as now. Ayesha, Hafsa, Ramlah, Sawdah, Zainab, Zainab, Maimunah, Safia, Juwairiyah, Umm Salimah the Makhzumite, Rehana the Jew, and the beautiful Mary the Copt.* Silently, they remain on their knees. Their wishes are made known to him without words. *What is an archangel but a puppet? Kathputli, marionette. The faithful bend us to their will. We are forces of nature and they, our masters. Mistresses, too. . . .*
He stands among the kneeling children, waiting for the pimps.
And when they come, he at last takes out, and presses to his lips, his unquiet horn: the exterminator, Azraeel. (460, author's emphasis)

At last, one feels, here is a link between the dream and the reality and a use of recurring names that makes sense, that means something. At a theological level what is often implied elsewhere in the book is stated openly here: That which humanity is pleased to call the supernatural in fact does what is required of it by humanity. At the social level Rushdie also gives satisfying expression to the reader's indignation at such ulcerous social evils as child prostitution and child abuse of all kinds. At the same time, moreover, he makes amends for his lapse of moral tone in the brothel episode, to which the passage is so closely linked. Prostitution appears here in its true colors.

Such gestures, however, are all too easily made. Almost everyone has longed to have some equivalent of Gibreel's Azraeel[31] to hand with which to "zap" those responsible for their frustrated outrage. But most people, including Rushdie, know how little the extermination of a few pimps will achieve beyond relieving their feelings. This, remember, is the Gibreel who would save London by changing its climate to that of Bombay, who drops his clothes all over Alleluia's apartment, who leaves the lives of Rekha Merchant, Alleluia Cone, and even Orphia Phillips worse than he found them—the all-too-human Gibreel. Rushdie is certainly holding up a mirror, of his own inimitable making, to a social evil. But such satire as there is is mainly of the well-meaning Gibreel in all of us.

Another unforgettable scene from that same night's events is the police raid on Club Hot Wax, the joint where, as the evening nears its climax and the patrons chant "Meltdown," wax effigies of hate objects such as Maggie Thatcher or Police Inspector Stephen Kinch are microwaved. What more obvious hotbed of disaffection and who knows what unspeakable practices? Cleverly, yet with Brechtian insistence that the audience remain aware of what he is doing, Rushdie presents the situation in the words of Inspector Kinch as he is interviewed on television and through the lenses of the cameras trained on him and the scene beyond—a scene over which a "helicopter hovers . . . urinating light in long golden streams." But a camera's "fragility makes it fastidious." It "requires law, order, the thin blue line" (454–55). The prose itself cuts from blackened wax corpses (carried out from the club as if for postmortem evidence) to a burning car to Inspector Kinch (pontificating on how lucky these kids are compared with their counterparts in Africa) to ambulances and stretchers to a television set in a store window narcissistically capturing an "infinite recession of television sets" (455–56). It is the aim and achievement of such writing to imitate but not to flatter the real-life presentation of such events as watched by the nation.

Ironically, in view of Rushdie's present situation, it is the police who throughout the novel are given a rougher ride than anyone else. This emphasis is most directly apparent in the account of how black leader Doctor Uhuru Simba screams out in the course of a nightmare while in custody awaiting trial and how police officers arrive just in time to see him fall to his death from the lower of the two bunks in his cell. The upper one is unaccountably unoccupied in a badly overcrowded jail. On a less serious level, while a brutish Saladin is being brutally conveyed to a detention center for illegal immigrants, he overhears the police discussing crowd-control tactics at football matches. These include feeding too rich a mixture to police horses the night before a big match, because showering spectators with shit always leads to violence, "*an' then we can really get amongst them, can't we just*" (162–63, author's emphasis). Later, when Pamela and Jumpy are robbed and murdered in a building that then burns down, readers are clearly intended to infer that the masked men who follow them into the building do so to recover documents implicating the police in witchcraft. Yet it is far from altogether naive of D. J. Enright to say of the second instance, as he might equally well have done of the third: "This could be an attack on police methods; it could be a sendup of right-minded attacks on police methods."[32] Neither caricature nor melodrama are without their weaknesses as instruments of satire.

Nor does Rushdie escape criticism for his treatment of those he purports to defend. Just as women may feel very ambivalent about the brothel episode, so some readers have responded negatively to what they perceive as condescension as well as inaccuracies in Rushdie's transliteration of West Indian speech patterns in the Orphia Phillips episode (328–31). There is no doubt, when judged by his articles, his interviews, and his account of a visit to Nicaragua in *The Jaguar Smile,* that Rushdie has the best of conscious intentions with respect to the need to do something about the gross inequalities of the world. But in his fiction, and particularly in *The Satanic Verses,* his unconscious attitudes may come through louder and clearer than those he intends to convey. This kind of writing is where an education as "preppy" and "ivy league" as is obtainable in Britain can be a handicap. Add perhaps a lingering lack of "house-training" such as Rushdie puts down to having servants around the house (*S.V.,* 310), plus just a trace of an Islamic and/or Indian attitude toward women, and there are almost bound to be failures of empathy and misjudgments of tone. Like the television cameras, he cannot help sometimes being on the wrong side of a "thin blue line."

Where he is more assured is in his treatment of some of the other successful members of the acquisitive society that his royalties keep him in touch with. Toward Billy Battuta he shows something of the amused admiration that Mishal and Anahita do when Saladin tells them the story of the fur coat (262–63). Like Dick Turpin, Ned Kelly, or Billy the Kid, Battuta does not even pretend to give to the poor what he takes from the rich; it is enough that he gets away with it. Hal Valance, the "creative half" of a cheerfully vulgar advertising agency, has even more gainful yet much less winning ways. As "creator of *The Aliens Show* and sole owner of the property, [he] took exactly seventeen seconds to congratulate Chamcha on being alive before beginning to explain why this fact did not affect the show's decision to dispense with his services" (264). From each of his first five independently wealthy wives he extracted a handsome divorce settlement, and the fact that his sixth is in the process of taking him for all he took from them does not really arouse our dormant sympathies. He exists like something Rushdie merely found, which is far from impossible—a self-created caricature of "philistine triumphalism," owner of "the first Loire chateau to be fitted with telex and fax machines" (266). Yet even Hal, even in his most egregiously racist moments, bears none of his victims any ill will. It is just a matter of their not fitting in with what the market demands any longer. The only real role he plays in the novel is as an exhibit in a gallery of grotesques;

like Browning's bishop ordering his tomb or duke ordering his next duchess, he is a specimen rather than a moral lesson.

So, despite what was said earlier about Rushdie "out-Swifting" Swift in his treatment of the Widow in *Midnight's Children,* it becomes increasingly clear in *The Satanic Verses* that Rushdie is not a true satirist at heart. Perhaps he does not hate hard enough. His genre is comedy—comic epic—as is Byron's in *Don Juan* or Garcia Marquez's in *One Hundred Years of Solitude.* All three authors have a satiric streak, of course. But mainly they write comedy out of a need to find grounds for laughter rather than despair. *The Satanic Verses* is the first Rushdie novel in which the comedy—comedy with a fortunate outcome, comedy that is an assertion of life even in the face of death—carries through right to the end.

Purity or Plenitude

The Satanic Verses is not, by Rushdie standards, innovative in its use of language. It holds the ground already won in the earlier novels but does not strike out into new territory. What it does do is explore new possibilities of structure. Structures there are in both *Midnight's Children* and *Shame,* buried under the plethora of incident and detail, but not such that one would necessarily notice them. That the chapters alternate, however, odd numbers one through nine devoted to reality and even numbers two through eight to dreams, is one of the most obvious structural features of *The Satanic Verses.* So a major critical problem to be resolved is the nature of the relationship between dream and reality. And the first thing to notice is that there is very little difference in their presentation apart, paradoxically, from the greater degree of realism to be found in the dreams. To be sure, the narration shifts its focus at will, now keeping us aware of the dreamer as well as the dream, now letting the dream unfold as if of its own accord. But then, these are inconsistencies or liberties of a kind any third-person omniscient narrator worth his salt (or any human being, for that matter, conducting the intermingled inner and outer, subjective and objective versions of his life) claims as a matter of course. No one in the dream episodes, however, falls unharmed for 29,002 feet, and the only manticores there are human revelers in fancy dress. It is as if Rushdie wishes to isolate the mystic encounters between Gibreel and Mahound, or Ayesha, or even the Imam, so as to protect them in a kind of reverse quarantine from being contaminated by the everyday magic of magic realism. Instead of the dreams being twice removed from reality, therefore, as Rushdie implies when describing them as "the fictional dream of a fictional character" in his letter to Rajiv Gandhi,[33] they have a greater measure of realism than the undreamed fiction. The fact that such realism, such authenticity, is used tellingly to imply the potentially dubious authenticity—that is, the subjectivity—of almost any revelation of divine truth is the one point on which Rushdie and all his critics are agreed.

The affirmative corollary of such skepticism is, of course, the salutary nature of doubt, flexibility, inclusiveness, and multiplicity, as opposed to the rigidity and exclusivity of revealed truth and the dogmas it spawns. Rushdie himself put it eloquently while defending *The Satanic Verses* against its detractors in a recent pronouncement:

Those who oppose the novel most vociferously today are of the opinion that intermingling with a different culture will inevitably weaken and ruin their own. I am of the opposite opinion. *The Satanic Verses* celebrates hybridity, impurity, intermingling, the transformation that comes of new and unexpected combinations of human beings, cultures, ideas, politics, movies, songs. It rejoices in mongrelization and fears the absolutism of the Pure. Mélange, hotch-potch, a bit of this and a bit of that is *how newness enters the world*. It is the great possibility that mass migration gives the world, and I have tried to embrace it. *The Satanic Verses* is for change-by-fusion, change-by-conjoining. It is a love-song to our mongrel selves.[34] (author's emphasis)

It is possible, though not everyone's choice, to see the hospitability that characterizes The Curtain as symbolic of just such tolerance, catholicity, and openness to the variety and variability of life. In the main, however, it is to the odd-numbered chapters that readers must turn to find such qualities exemplified. There, as already noted, each character satirized, whether Hal Valance, Inspector Kinch, or Billy Battuta, is also a new exhibit in the Rushdie waxworks of human oddity. In addition and in even greater abundance there is the usual Dickensian array of such minor characters as (to name only female ones) Zeenat Vakil, Rekha Merchant, Rosa Diamond, Pamela Chamcha, Mimi Mamoulin, Mishal and Hind Sufyan, and Alicja Cone. (In this respect as in many others, *The Satanic Verses* harks back to *Midnight's Children* rather than *Shame*.)

As if to signal the advent of this quality in the remainder of the novel, moreover, there are two key statements in favor of hybridity in its opening chapter or section. First, Zeenat Vakil, Saladin's Indian lover, is not only a doctor but "an art critic whose book on the confining myth of authenticity, that folkloristic straitjacket which she sought to replace by an ethic of historically validated eclecticism, for was not the entire national culture based on the principle of borrowing whatever clothes seemed to fit, Aryan, Mughal,

British, take-the-best-and-leave-the-rest?—had created a predictable stink"
(52). Second, Changez ("Mutability"?) Chamchawala, Saladin's father, has
a priceless collection of *Hamza-nama* paintings dating from when the
"Mughals had brought artists from every part of India to work on the paintings." Each picture was the work of a team of artists, each painting in his
own style, yet "individual identity was submerged to create a many-headed,
many-brushed Overartist who, literally, *was* Indian painting" thereby providing "eloquent proof of Zeeny Vakil's thesis about the eclectic, hybridized
nature of Indian artistic tradition" (70).[35]

In some ways all of Rushdie's novels, taken together, compose a paean of
praise to variety and illustrate Elfrida Gribb's contention in *Grimus,* and
Rushdie's later assertion in an interview, that fiction should leave room for
loose ends to suggest its attempt to be inclusive.[36] But it is *Midnight's
Children*—implicitly Hindu in its inclusiveness and in the multitalentedness
of the children themselves—and *The Satanic Verses*—implicitly and explic-
itly inclusive in its emphasis on migration, metamorphosis, and mongrelization, its multimedia dream-and-reality presentation, and its rejection of
exclusive intolerance—that most obviously celebrate the whole range of
possibilities open to human beings just by being human. That is why
Rushdie's return to the big canvas, after the more restricted negativism of
Shame, is so important; it reaffirms his belief in the variety and the variability needed to maintain a sufficiently diversified gene and idea pool. This,
then, is the key to the profound if often less than apparent interrelatedness
of dream and reality in the novel. Rushdie may resort to repetition of
names, may even have foisted angelic and satanic roles on Gibreel and
Saladin, in order to maintain a surface appearance of a unified novel. But
far more important than such mere expedients is the juxtaposition within
the novel of richness and sterility, fixity and flux. For fundamentalism of
any kind and the conformity and rigidity it attempts to impose on its followers are the sworn enemies of all forms of pluralism, of variety and
variability—of the processes and essence of life itself.

This is as true of Dumsday and his denunciation of Darwin as of the
imam with his hatred of history; both, though to differing degrees of intensity, are fundamentalism incarnate. Moreover, though Mahound and the
village girl Ayesha differ appreciably from the imam, each has a similar core
of stubborn rigidity. That said, however, one should qualify the assertion as
it applies to Mahound. Twice the poet Baal asks of Mahound and his new
religion: "*What kind of an idea are you?*" (author's emphasis). The answers
he receives differ. When "Submission" (or Islam) is in its infancy, or weak, it
must remain rigid and unyielding if it is to have any chance of changing the

world. But when it is securely established and strong, it can afford to be flexible and even forgiving. So when Mahound considers acknowledging the three goddesses Lat, Manat, and Uzza as having subsidiary divine status, it is necessary that he should revert to uncompromising monotheism by denouncing the compromise as satanically inspired. But when he returns as conquering hero to Mecca, he can afford to spare Salman and even Hind (though not Baal!), and indeed he strengthens his position by showing himself able to do so.

In this way, while acknowledging Muhammad's need to be uncompromisingly single-minded and even ruthless in the early stages of his prophetic mission, Rushdie demonstrates that he moved in the direction of flexibility and tolerance—that his whole life offers, in fact, an example of controlled but increasing mutability. How one applies such an interpretation of the Prophet's life to the contemporary situation will vary, of course. On the one hand, Islam is among the world's few major religions —a religion, moreover, that is gaining converts and expanding at a faster rate than any of its rivals. It is therefore powerful enough to be more tolerant and flexible. On the other hand, however, Islam is predominantly a religion of the third world. After a period of glory in the centuries following Muhammad's life, when at one time or another, politically and economically as well as religiously, it controlled much of the world from Spain to Indonesia, it has seen its power, influence, and territory usurped by European imperialism. So recently have most Islamic states escaped from such bondage, and so lacking still is most of the Islamic world in either economic or military power, that many feel Islam to be once more in a position where it needs to be inflexible. With that position Rushdie clearly disagrees profoundly. So may most of his and my readers. But they should remember that, to his opponents, this dissension is only to be expected of one who has chosen to become a citizen of what was until recently the world's most successful exponent of such imperialism.

Finally, it is possible to see the incident of the satanic verses as being positive in itself rather than merely negative. Even the most orthodox of Muslims must surely acknowledge, provided they see Muhammad as the *human* bearer of divine glad tidings, that the story can be read as being about a cleverly presented, plausible temptation that is eventually resisted. That it was successfully resisted, however, is probably less important than that it was ever entertained. Authentic or not, the story illustrates the potential flexibility of someone confident enough in his strength of purpose to dare to contemplate change. Most important of all, it shows the process of divine inspiration (however one interprets those words) as being shot through with such human factors as judgment, choice, changing interpretations, and the need for the divine to be accessible, comprehensible, and challenging to the current conceptual range of different individuals and societies. Such a vision will always be disconcerting, terrifying even, to those who need their faith as a reassuring refuge of absolute and immutable certainties. But such is the vision that Rushdie insists on presenting to his readers, not as a threat but as a promise of richness and potential. To see the deity on the one hand as intrinsically unchanging throughout eternity and on the other as forever changing and expanding, insofar as the human mind and its capacity to comprehend the divine changes and expands, is surely the only way of not insulting the infinite and eternal by tying everything down to the puny measure of human understanding at any one stage in its development.

Chapter Seven
Conclusion

Salman Rushdie is a world writer. One can say as much by virtue not just of his qualities as a writer, which are many and important, but also of his belonging to a number of overlapping clusters, cliques, or concatenations of authors. There is first the growing number of Commonwealth writers— that is, those who, neither British nor American, write in English and come from countries that are or were members of the British Commonwealth. These include, among many others, Elizabeth Jolley and Patrick White from Australia, Margaret Atwood and Alice Munro from Canada, Wilson Harris and George Lamming from the Caribbean, Anita Desai and R. K. Narayan from India, Janet Frame and Maurice Shadbolt from New Zealand, Chinua Achebe and Wole Soyinka from Nigeria, and J. M. Coetzee and Nadine Gordimer from South Africa. A number of these also belong to a large group of third-world novelists from Latin America, Africa, and Asia, many of whom write in a colonialist language, such as Spanish, French, or English, and of whom Naguib Mahfouz of Egypt, as the first Muslim as well as the first writer in Arabic to win a Nobel Prize, is of particular interest in connection with Rushdie. Writers belonging to both the above groups with whom Rushdie might have been expected to show particular affinities, but from whom he has been at some pains to distance himself, are Indian novelists writing in English. With the exception of G. V. Desani's *All About H. Hatterr,* their work has little in common with his, he feels, and has had little influence other than a negative one on his output. What seems to set him apart more than anything else from his compatriots is his more innovative and adventurous use of language.

Next there is the group of expatriates, like Milan Kundera (from Czechoslovakia, living in France), Mavis Gallant (from Canada, living in France), Ruth Prawer Jhabvala (a child in Germany, a student in England, a wife and mother in India, and now a resident for much of the year in the United States), Bharati Mukherjee (from India, living in the United States), V. S. Naipaul (from Trinidad, living in England), and Michael Ondaatje (from Sri Lanka, living in Canada). Never have there been so many writers with new, improvised, or borrowed roots. Rushdie, with his emphasis on migration and mongrelization, is clearly a founding member of this group.

Finally and probably of greatest importance to Rushdie as an artist, there are the novelists he so often acknowledges as having strongly influenced him and about whose fiction he has in most cases written. These include Jorge Borges, Gabriel Garcia Marquez, Günter Grass, Milan Kundera, and Thomas Pynchon. All employ the self-conscious, metafictional strategies of postmodernism (as of course did Laurence Sterne, another of Rushdie's role models), and several of them work for the most part in a "large-scale, fantasized, satiric, anti-epic tradition" of the kind to be found in Rushdie's works and, as he acknowledges, those of "Rabelais or Gogol or Boccaccio."[1]

One author who also appears on the Commonwealth, third-world, and expatriate list of names, who also has an Indian heritage from which he is even farther removed than Rushdie, is V. S. Naipaul. Escaping from Trinidad, whither his family had escaped from India two generations earlier, he studied at Oxford as Rushdie did at Cambridge. After Oxford he became, like Rushdie, a Londoner. As Rushdie uses the Indian subcontinent as the setting for *Midnight's Children* and *Shame,* so Naipaul uses the Caribbean as the locale for much or all of novels such as *A House for Mr Biswas* and *The Mimic Men,* the first of which includes a good deal of autobiographical material. Like Rushdie's, moreover, Naipaul's fiction usually has strong social and political implications, though not in the form of a roman à clef like *Shame.* Later novels, however, such as *In a Free State* and *A Bend in the River,* both set in central Africa, are nearer to the blend of the historical and the fictional that Rushdie serves us in his Indian novels. Despite many similarities, however, it is the differences between these two authors that are far more illuminating. In Naipaul's work the mode is always realistic, never fantastic. Sometimes, indeed, the line between his numerous travel books and his equally numerous novels becomes a little fuzzy. The style is always restrained, ironic, and unobtrusive, and the narrative techniques traditional and unostentatious.

Both authors have aroused deep resentment on the part of those they have presumed to criticize, as much for the patrician air they are perceived to have adopted as for what they actually write in their books. Chinua Achebe among others is fiercely critical of the despairing picture of Zaire (formerly the Belgian Congo, of which Conrad wrote in *Heart of Darkness*) that Naipaul paints in *A Bend in the River.*[2] And Rushdie's postcolonial credentials are suspect, even apart from the anger that *The Satanic Verses* has provoked in the Muslim world. When Naipaul writes directly and quite critically of the Muslim world, however, as in *Among the Believers: An Islamic Journey,* he runs no risk of a fatal fatwa. This immunity is partly because he is not a Muslim (his ancestry is a Hindu one) but mainly because his tone is never flippantly disrespectful. Rather, he maintains an impecca- bly uninvolved tone, producing fiction and travelogue, travelogue and fic- tion in roughly the same-sized slices, as the occasion demands, and evincing a mild but increasingly unrelieved pessimism, not to say misanthropy, in re- lation to more and more of the earth's surface and inhabitants.

Rushdie, by contrast, is a much more involved author. Either in his own person or in that of his narrator, he is an importunate, badgering presence in his fiction. He clearly wants to share the "look-no-hands-mom" pleasure he gets from using metafictional and other attention-grabbing techniques. In citing *The Marriage of Heaven and Hell* as one of the two most important literary influences on *The Satanic Verses,* he may have been consciously thinking of it as "the classic meditation on the interpenetration of good and evil,"[3] but in almost everything he writes he is also clearly in agreement with Blake that "the road of excess leads to the palace of wisdom." The prose alone, with all its excesses, tells us that it was not written by a man sliding gently but irrevocably into misanthropic despair. This is writing of broad, brash, Romantic excess, but in a comic mode. Ultimately almost everything one can say about Rushdie's novels is exemplified in his prose style.

It is the prose too, I have argued, that most clearly sets Rushdie apart from his fellow Indian novelists. And it is the prose style, the narrative voice, the postmodern metafictional devices, and the magic-realist commitment to the comic mode that link him to the novelists to which he feels closest. Whether it be Pynchon's page-long sentences, the comical mock-epical magical realism of Garcia Marquez, the unbearable lightness of Milan Kundera's laughter and forgetting, or the barely contained anger within Günter Grass's grotesques, something similar can be found in Rushdie.

As for Rushdie's message, the only area of postcolonialist doctrine in which he cannot be faulted is once again linguistic and stylistic. In his flag- waving "The Empire Writes Back with a Vengeance"[4] he makes the virtu- ally canonic claim that the English language is being reshaped and in the process reinvigorated by its new colonial users, as it has been in the past by Irish and American writers. When it comes to analyzing the residually harmful heritage of or the damage still being wrought by colonialist exploi- tation, however, both Rushdie and Saladin Chamcha are equally in danger of being regarded as brown Uncle Toms. The latter sings the praises of hos- pitable England and asks, "Would the United States, with its are-you-now- have-you-ever-beens, have permitted Ho Chi Minh to cook in its hotel kitchens?" (398–99), and the former affectionately allows him to do so with only a trace of irony.

But upon what compulsion, as Falstaff might ask, must Rushdie meet the criteria for salvation specified by some postcolonial catechism? May not Rushdie's *Shame,* equally with Swift's *A Modest Proposal,* concentrate on convincing its readers that something is rotten in the state of Pakistan or Ireland or the world without analyzing the root causes? Isn't diagnosing the disease as valid a literary function as apportioning blame for bringing infection into the house?

The one novel in which, to his discomfiture, Rushdie has been at all specific about what went wrong and when and where it did so is *The Satanic Verses.* Even there, however, it is only implied that the relative fluidity of Islam at its inception—the freedom to think God has told you one thing and then to realize your mistake and have Him tell you another—has been replaced by rigidity. What is also implicit in all of Rushdie's work—though more specifically and more abundantly in *Midnight's Children* and *The Satanic Verses* than in the other novels—and what is explicit in an extract quoted above from *In Good Faith* and in other polemical prose pieces is the need he sees for the maximum flexibility, variety, variability, and intermingling or "hybridity" of human ideas and beliefs and customs. This belief comes in part from his strong sense of how much immigrants have contributed in the past and will continue to do so in the future to such mixed cultures as those of India and Britain—and indeed to almost all cultures. It is also the product of his knowing how much of a threat to the values of societies that put a premium on tolerance and the free exchange of ideas is posed by the contrary values of regimes preaching purity of race and fixity of doctrine and practicing persecution of nonconformity. In addition, there is an intriguingly nineteenth-century, Darwinian quality to his emphasis on variety and metamorphosis or changeability, especially in view of the scattered references to Darwin and Lamarck in the novel. Darwinism as applied to human affairs has too often led to racism and determinism, but it can of course be seen as confirming the nineteenth-century belief in the absolute freedom for ideas to compete with one another so as to ensure, through natural selection, the survival of the fittest or best.[5] Such faith in intellectual laissez-faire will naturally horrify not only followers of the Ayatollah but also doctrinaire followers of anyone or anything. So be it.

As a writer who exemplifies both excess and variety, Rushdie is almost bound, like a seventeen-course meal, to offend the taste of someone. A more prudent author would have recognized the brothel episode in *The Satanic Verses,* for instance, as offering a relatively small gain in comedy, a somewhat confused message as to its significance, and a maximum likelihood of giving offense. A tidier or more timid author would not have risked mixing fact and fiction, wakefulness and dreams, realism and fantasy, all in the same story. A less reckless author would not have used humor to question the dearest religious convictions of many millions. But Rushdie is not a prudent, tidy, timid author. He is a very passionate author, every bit as passionate and sincere as any of his detractors, and both his passion and his convictions are an integral part of the books he writes—of their style just as much as of the characters and events they depict.

It also may well be true that he is somewhat naive in his understanding and expectations of the great mass of his fellow mortals. He writes recently, for instance: "It has been bewildering to learn that people, millions upon millions of people, have been willing to judge *The Satanic Verses* and its author, without reading it, without finding out what manner of man this fellow might be. . . . It has been bewildering to learn that people *do not care about art*" (author's emphasis).[6] Clearly he has not had to deal with parents objecting to their children having to study *Catcher in the Rye* or *The Stone Angel* in school—people who are equally willing to condemn books they have not read and who seem incapable of reading and judging a work as a totality rather than as half a dozen isolated well-thumbed pages. Clearly he has forgotten how difficult it was for Joyce and Lawrence to have their novels judged as art rather than pornography. Perhaps he has even forgotten the problems experienced by Christ or Muhammad in trying to gain acceptance for their new visions of life.

In comparing his case with theirs I am paying him the compliment—the well-deserved compliment—of taking his work very seriously. To do so it is essential to view it as a whole. And by that I mean not merely reading *The Satanic Verses* or any of the other novels all the way through but also seeing the characters, the plot, the prose style, the mode of narration, the tone, everything about the books, as parts of a whole—ingredients whose flavors leak into one another during the complex "chutnification" of Rushdie's particular brand of fiction. "To understand me," his work tells us, "you'll have to swallow a world."

Notes and References

Preface

    1. Announcement on Teheran Radio of the *fatwa* (i.e., legal ruling in answer to a request for such) by the Ayatollah Khomeini on the alleged blasphemy and apostasy vis-à-vis Islam of the author of *The Satanic Verses,* cited by Malise Ruthven in *A Satanic Affair: Salman Rushdie and the Rage of Islam* (London: Chatto & Windus, 1990), 112, and also in *The Rushdie File,* ed. Lisa Appignanesi and Sara Maitland (Syracuse: Syracuse University Press, 1990), 68.

    2. *The Rushdie File,* 92, 139.

    3. Said here uses the older, more familiar transliteration of the word most of my sources, including Rushdie, spell *Muhammad.* Similarly, he uses *Moslem* to their *Muslim.*

    4. Edward W. Said, *Orientalism* (New York: Vintage, 1979), 72.

    5. *The Rushdie File,* 165.

    6. *The Rushdie File,* 164–65.

    7. Salman Rushdie, "Outside the Whale," *Granta* 11 (1983): 123–41.

Chapter One

    1. John Haffenden, *Novelists in Interview* (London: Methuen, 1985), 233.

    2. "The Marked Man: A Writer Driven by Life to Dissent," *Sunday Times,* 19 February 1989, cited in *The Rushdie File,* 2.

    3. Haffenden, *Novelists in Interview,* 233–34.

    4. Haffenden, *Novelists in Interview,* 235.

    5. *The Rushdie File,* 3.

    6. Haffenden, *Novelists in Interview,* 235–36.

    7. Haffenden, *Novelists in Interview,* 236–37.

    8. "A national literature is one that takes the whole nation for its province. . . . An ethnic literature is one which is available only to one ethnic group within the nation. If you take Nigeria as an example, the national literature, as I see it, is the literature written in English; and the ethnic literatures are in Hausa, Ibo, Yoruba, Efik, Edo, Ijaw, etc., etc." Chinua Achebe, *Morning Yet on Creation Day* (London: Heinemann, 1975), 56.

    9. Stated at a panel discussion at the Harborfront Literary Festival in Toronto, October 1988, in answer to a questioner wanting to know why he writes in English.

    10. Salman Rushdie and Cecile Wajsbrot, "Utiliser une technique qui permette à Dieu d'exister," *Quinzaine Littéraire,* no. 449 (1985): 22.

    11. Salman Rushdie, "Interview," *Kunapipi* 4, no. 2 (1982): 19.

12. *New Society* (9 December 1982): 417–20; *Guardian,* 3 May 1983; *Guardian,* 3 December 1984.

13. See Feroza Jussawalla, "Resurrecting the Prophet: The Case of Salman, the Otherwise," *Public Culture* 2, no. 1 (1989), 114, and Timothy Brennan, *Salman Rushdie and the Third World* (London: Macmillan), 164.

14. *The Jaguar Smile* (London: Pan Books, 1987), 13 (hereafter cited in text).

15. Ruthven, *A Satanic Affair,* 86. See also *The Rushdie File,* 28, 30–32.

16. *The Rushdie File,* 28.

17. "Rushdie's book is a godsend to those who, in the name of the defence of an offended Islam, dream of taking control in the West of communities who are often disoriented, badly integrated, both in social and religious terms." From *Le Monde,* 28 February 1989, quoted in *The Rushdie File,* 132.

18. Ruthven, *A Satanic Affair,* 111.

19. Malcolm Yapp, "The Hubris of the Hidden Imam," *Independent,* 22 February 1989; quoted in *The Rushdie File,* 91–94.

20. *Irna (Iranian News Agency),* 19 February 1989, quoted in *The Rushdie File,* 99.

21. Gerald Marzorati, "Rushdie in Hiding: An Interview," *New York Times Magazine,* 4 November 1990, 68.

22. Marzorati, "Rushdie in Hiding," 78.

23. Marzorati, "Rushdie in Hiding," 68, 78.

24. "Rushdie Seeks to Mend His Rift with Islam: The Writer's Statement," *New York Times,* 25 December 1990, 26.

25. "No Iranian Forgiveness for Salman Rushdie," *New York Times,* 27 December 1990, 13, 20.

Chapter Two

1. Wajsbrot and Rushdie, "Utiliser une technique qui permette à Dieu d'exister," 22.

2. Offensive to Hindus and/or Muslims respectively, cows being sacred to the former and pigs unclean to the latter.

3. *Midnight's Children* (New York: Alfred A. Knopf, 1981), 35–36 (hereafter cited in text as *M.C.*)

4. In a recent interview Rushdie revealed that one of the "sacred objects" he managed to take into hiding with him was "a little inch-high block of silver, Indian silver, engraved with the map of the unpartitioned continent of India and Pakistan, which was given to me as a present by a friend of my father's when I was one day old. It is my oldest possession, so it goes everywhere with me." *Newsweek,* 12 February 1990, 48.

5. W. Norman Brown, *The United States and India, Pakistan, Bangladesh* (Cambridge, Mass.: Harvard University Press, 1972), 160.

6. "There is a Sanscrit word, *pashanda,* which is translated into English as 'heretic', but it only means a person who is un-Hindu in his conduct and behaviour,

who neglects Hindu observances, and disregards Hindu taboos. It is not possible to find doctrinal heresy in Hinduism because Hinduism has no fixed doctrine." Nirad C. Chaudhuri, *Hinduism* (New York: Oxford University Press, 1979), 148.

7. Sarvepalli Radhakrishnan and Charles A. Moore, eds., *A Sourcebook in Indian Philosophy* (Princeton: Princeton University Press, 1957), xviii.

8. "Hinduism," *Encyclopaedia Britannica,* 15th ed., 20, 582.

9. "On one occasion, when the gods were churning the ocean with the aid of a mountain and a giant snake in order to create the liquid of immortality, and Vishnu in his avatar form of a turtle was stabilizing the whole operation by acting as the pivot for the rotating mountain, the strain on the snake caused it to vent torrents of venom over the whole earth. It was Shiva who saved mankind by swallowing the poison and burning his throat in the process." P. Masson-Oursel and Louise Morin, "Indian Mythology" in *New Larousse Encyclopedia of Mythology,* 2d ed. (London: Hamlyn, 1983), 362–67.

10. These are the three names under which she is commonly worshiped. *Larousse* (375) amplifies the list. "The feminine divinity which personifies the 'power' (Sakti) of Siva [Shiva] is Parvati, daughter of the Himalayas, also named Uma, the gracious, and Bhairavi, the terrible, Ambika the generatrix, Sati the good wife [Sati, according to one myth, is Parvati in a previous incarnation], Gauri the brilliant, Kali the black, Durga the inaccessible."

11. See Romila Thapar, *A History of India,* vol. 1 (London: Penguin, 1966), 133, 263; *Larousse,* 378; Wendy Doniger O'Flaherty, *Hindu Myths* (Harmondsworth: Penguin, 1975), 261–69. Rushdie's own version of the Ganesh story differs from all of the above and, as he explains, fits Saleem's case even better. "The legend of Ganesh is the legend of disputed parentage; that's to say the reason he has the head of an elephant is because Shiva and Parvati quarrel over who the father of the child is. Shiva becomes convinced that his wife has been fooling around, that this child is not his, and so in rage he cuts off its head and then, repenting, looks around heaven for a head; and what comes to hand is the head of an elephant. This is stuck on, and so you have a god with an elephant's head. Now it seemed to me that since Saleem's entire ancestry is also very murky and disputed. . . ." Salman Rushdie, "*Midnight's Children* and *Shame,*" *Kunapipi* 8, no. 1 (1984): 9.

12. In the *Bhagavadgita,* Krishna expounds the threefold path to final liberation in the course of persuading a reluctant Prince Arjuna that he is justified in doing his duty as a member of the warrior caste in the forthcoming battle, even if he kills friends and relatives, since none of them will really die.

13. Thapar, *History of India,* 37–39.

14. Consider the letter to "MISS PROBLEM-WALLA, c/o EVE'S BEAUT14.Y-BASKET, BOMBAY-1" in Bharati Mukherjee's *Wife* (New York: Penguin, 1987), page 10, which begins: "I am a young woman of twenty with wheatish complexion." Also consider the advertisement in Ruth Prawer Jhabvala's *The Nature of Passion* (Harmondsworth: Penguin, 1986), page 13: "*Wanted, for Punjabi boy, 21, wheat complexion, B.A., first-class family, a beautiful fair girl . . .*"

Similarly, in *Midnight's Children,* Ahmed Sinai looks at the dark-skinned Mumtaz and thinks: "This girl, I never looked at her, but my goodness me. . . . Well, never mind about the skin . . ."(63).

15. Malise Ruthven, *Islam in the World* (New York: Oxford University Press, 1984), 117–20, 198–99.

16. See Maxime Rodinson, *Muhammad,* tr. Anne Carter (New York: Pantheon Books, 1980), 106–107; W. Montgomery Watt, *Muhammad, Prophet and Statesman* (London: Oxford University Press, 1961), 60–65; Ruthven, *A Satanic Affair,* 37–39.

17. Ruthven, *A Satanic Affair,* 39, citing the opinion of John Burton in "Those Are the High-Flying Cranes," *Journal of Semitic Studies* 15 (1970): 246 ff.

18. "Whether or not Muhammad became more adept at 'calling up' revelations in order to deal with the demands of the moment, the Quranic passages dating from the Medinese period are mostly of a different character from that of the ecstatic utterances of the early Meccan years. The Quran becomes more conscious of itself as a source of law and as a commentary on current events." Ruthven, *Islam in the World,* 71–72.

19. "Islamic doctrine, law, and thinking in general are based upon four sources, or fundamental principles: (1) the Quran, (2) the *sunnah* ("traditions"), (3) *ijma* ("consensus"), and (4) *ijtihad* ("individual thought"). . . . From the 3rd century AH [9th century A.D.] *ijma* has amounted to a principle of rigidity in thinking; points on which consensus was reached in practice were considered closed and further substantial questioning of them prohibited. . . . *Ijtihad,* meaning "to endeavour" or "to exert effort," was required to find the legal or doctrinal solution to a new problem. In the early period of Islam, because *ijtihad* took the form of individual opinion (*ra'y*), there was a wealth of conflicting and chaotic opinions. In the 2nd century AH *ijtihad* was replaced by *giyas* (reasoning by strict analogy), a formal procedure of deduction based on the texts of the Quran and the Hadith [an authorized collection of sayings attributed to the Prophet]. The transformation of *ijma* into a conservative mechanism and the acceptance of a definitive body of Hadith virtually closed the 'gate of *ijtihad.*' " "Islam," *Encyclopaedia Britannica* 15th ed., vol. 22, 5.

20. Ruthven, *Islam in the World,* 187 ff.

21. Brown, *U.S.A. and India,* 150.

22. Brown, *U.S.A. and India,* 233–34.

23. *Shame* (New York: Alfred A. Knopf, 1983), 120 (hereafter cited in text). Pagination is identical to that of the 1989 Vintage International edition.

24. Rushdie, "*Midnight's Children* and *Shame,*" 18–19.

25. Percival Spear, *History of India,* vol. 2 (London: Penguin, 1965), 262–63.

Chapter Three

1. *Grimus* (Woodstock, N.Y.: The Overlook Press, 1982), 77 (hereafter cited in text). The anagrams exhibited here are not to be taken as examples of Gorfic skill at its best.

2. Logically this passage should settle the issue as to whether Calf Island and other Endimions were "found" or "made," since if they were "found" they had clearly existed before being equipped with the "Object" without which, it transpires, they cannot continue to exist. But one is not entirely confident that Rushdie has worked everything out in such detail.

3. Hugh Everett III, " 'Relative State' Formulation of Quantum Mechanics," *Reviews of Modern Physics* 29, no. 3 (1957): 454–62, reprinted, with an epigraph from Jorge Luis Borges's "The Garden of Forking Paths," in *The Many-Worlds Interpretation of Quantum Mechanics,* ed. Bryce S. DeWitt and Neill Graham (Princeton: Princeton University Press, 1973), 141–49. Everett argues that, when a quantum may do either of two things and seems to do both, it *does* do both, one in this universe and one in another, though none of these "many worlds" can communicate with each other.

4. Salman Rushdie, letter to author, 29 March 1988.

5. Rushdie, "Outside the Whale," 130.

6. Karl Marx, *Criticism of the Gotha Program,* cited in *The Oxford Dictionary of Quotations,* 2d ed. (London: Oxford University Press, 1953), 333.

7. Rushdie, "*Midnight's Children* and *Shame,*" 17–18.

8. As Rushdie himself explains things: "In the poem ["The Conference of Birds"] twenty-nine birds are persuaded by a hoopoe, a messenger of a bird god, to make a pilgrimage to the god. They set off and go through allegorical valleys and eventually climb the mountain to meet the god at the top, but at the top they find that there is no god there. The god is called Simurg, and they accuse the hoopoe of bringing them on—oh dear—a wild goose chase. The whole poem rests on a Persian pun: if you break Simurg into parts—'Si' and 'murg'—it can be translated to mean 'thirty birds', so that, having gone through the process of purification and reached the top of the mountain, the birds have become the god" (Haffenden, *Novelists in Interview,* 245). The same legend is referred to in *Shame* in the form of "an exquisitely carved walnut screen on which was portrayed the mythical circular mountain of Qaf, complete with the thirty birds playing god thereupon" (29).

9. Haffenden, *Novelists in Interview,* 239.

10. Fawzi Afzal-Khan, "Post-Modernist Strategies of Liberation in the Works of Salman Rushdie," *Journal of South Asian Literature* 23 (1988): 143.

11. Uma Parameswaran, "Handcuffed to History: Salman Rushdie's Art," *Ariel* 14, no. 4 (1983): 37.

12. Rushdie, "*Midnight's Children* and *Shame,*" 3.

13. Whether Grimus and his helpers found or made the "paradise, fertile, lush and green" that Calf Island started out as (211) is almost theological in its unresolvable irrelevance, as is whether Gorf Koax found or created the life forms (and their Endimions?) of the universe. He is the efficient if not the absolute cause of the links between them—and awarenesses of each other—that make possible and indeed constitute the world of *Grimus*—the God, if you will, of *Grimus*. The only acts of creation about which Rushdie is unequivocal are those resulting from Virgil

Jones's discovery that "one could *create* worlds, physical, external worlds, neither aspects of oneself nor a palimpsest-universe. Fictions where a man could live. In those days, Mr. Jones had been a highly imaginative man" (91).

Mr. Rushdie, too, is a highly imaginative man. Whether or not gods create, he knows that artists do.

14. "Their origins are lost in mystery; some radiation, perhaps, blasting their now-barren planet, formed the rock into these masterpieces of intelligence and at the same time trapped them in the tragic irony of near-immobility and total isolation" (65).

Chapter Four

1. Brennan, *Salman Rushdie and the Third World,* 152–53.

2. To readers of cricket-playing nationalities, of course, the "M.C.C." is the Marylebone Cricket Club, a London club that grew like Topsy to become the governing body of English cricket.

3. Haffenden, *Novelists in Interview,* 239.

4. Be it noted that when, at the end of the chapter "A Wedding" (406), Rushdie finally identifies "the Widow" as Indira Gandhi and devotes a paragraph to a biographical note, "just in case you had failed to realize that the Prime Minister of India was, in 1975, fifteen years a widow," he refers at some length to her son, Sanjay Gandhi (killed in a plane accident in 1980). The paragraph's closing sentence reads: "The Sanjay Youth Movement was particularly effective in the sterilization campaign." What that campaign promoted were "the simple vas- and tubectomies" that were not used in the case of the children of midnight, though the vigor with which (perhaps understandably, in view of India's birthrate) Sanjay pursued the campaign led to much bitter criticism. One suspects, however, that Rushdie's venom is reserved for the Widow herself and that he has merely used the nature and ardor of Sanjay's crusade as a metaphor for hers.

5. Rushdie, "*Midnight's Children* and *Shame,*" 10.

6. Haffenden, *Novelists in Interview,* 239.

7. Richard Cronin, "The Indian English Novel: *Kim* and *Midnight's Children,*" *Modern Fiction Studies* 33, no. 2 (1987): 201.

8. See also, among others, pages 20, 45–46, 87, 106–108, 232–33, 270–71, 331–32, 339–40, 353–54, 364–65, 369–70, 372, 391–92, 435–36, and 445.

9. See also *M.C.,* 207, 320, 365, 388, and *Shame,* 99.

10. Rushdie, "*Midnight's Children* and *Shame,*" 10–11.

11. Radhakrishnan and Moore, *Sourcebook in Indian Philosophy,* xxviii.

12. For instance, C. Kanaganayakam, "Myth and Fabulosity in *Midnight's Children,*" *Dalhousie Review* 67 (1987): 88–92, or Deiter Reimenschneider, "History and the Individual in Anita Desai's *Clear Light of Day* and Salman Rushdie's *Midnight's Children,*" *World Literature Written in English* 23 (1984): 201–205.

13. Rushdie, "*Midnight's Children* and *Shame,*" 3.

14. John Stephens, " 'To tell the truth, I lied. . . .': Retrospectivity and Deconstruction as (Contributing) Strategies for Reading Salman Rushdie's *Midnight's Children,*" in *The Given Condition: Essays in Post Colonial Literature,* ed. Peter Simpson (SPAN, no. 21, Christchurch, New Zealand, 1985), 196–97 (hereafter cited as "Retrospectivity and Deconstruction").

15. Stephens, "Retrospectivity and Deconstruction," 195.

16. Rushdie, "*Midnight's Children* and *Shame,*" 2–3.

17. Rushdie, "*Midnight's Children* and *Shame,*" 6–8.

18. "For me, the special interest in this work is the role the author himself plays in the story. Vyasa not only composed the narrative, but being aware of the past and future of all his characters, helps them with solutions when they find themselves in a dilemma. Sometimes he may see into the future and emphasize the inevitability of certain coming events, making his heroes resign themselves to their fate." R. K. Narayan, Introduction to *The Mahabharata: A Shortened Modern Prose Version of the Indian Epic,* tr. R. K. Narayan (New York: Viking, 1978), xii.

19. Gabriel Garcia Marquez, *One Hundred Years of Solitude,* tr. Gregory Rabassa (New York: Harper & Row, 1970), 242–43 and 305–307.

20. The list is expanded and adapted from the one in Kumkum Sangari's "The Politics of the Possible: The Narrative Modes of Gabriel Garcia Marquez and Salman Rushdie," *Cultural Critique,* no. 7 (1987): 158.

21. Compare Saleem's analysis with Coleridge's of his role in *Lyrical Ballads* ("[I]t was agreed that my endeavors should be directed to persons and characters supernatural, or at least romantic; yet so as to transfer from our inward nature a human interest and a semblance of truth sufficient to procure for these shadows of imagination that willing suspension of disbelief for the moment, which constitutes poetic faith") and Wordsworth's ("to give the charm of novelty to things of every day, and to excite a feeling analogous to the supernatural, by awakening the mind's attention from the lethargy of custom and directing it to the loveliness and the wonders of the world before us"). *Biographia Literaria,* ed. James Engell and W. Jackson Bate, vol. 2, Vol. 7 of *The Collected Works of Samuel Taylor Coleridge* (Princeton: Princeton University Press, 1983), 6–7.

22. Rushdie, "*Midnight's Children* and *Shame,*" 6–7.

23. Salman Rushdie, "On Günter Grass," *Granta,* no. 15 (Spring 1985): 180. N.B. Gabriel Garcia Marquez's *Cien anos de soledad* was first published in Buenos Aires in 1967; its translation, *One Hundred Years of Solitude,* did not appear until 1970.

24. Said, *Orientalism,* 4–9 and passim.

25. Bruno Bettelheim, *The Uses of Enchantment* (New York: Vintage Books, 1977), 130–31, 140–41.

26. Rushdie, "Interview," *Kunapipi,* 23.

27. Arjuna, 74, 196; Bhima, 196; Brama, 207; Ganesh, 93, 129, 149, 154, 192; Ganga, 176; Hanuman, 84–85; Kali, 196, 355; Krishna, 103, 111,

136; Rama, 84, 196; the *Ramayana,* 149; Ravana, 84, 238; Shiva, 128, 216, 347; Shiva-lingam, 174, 270.

28. Rushdie, *"Midnight's Children* and *Shame,"* 2–3.

29. Quoted by Rustom Bharucha in "Rushdie's Whale" (*Massachusetts Review* 27 [1986]: 225) as an example of Rushdie's ability to draw on words from a variety of sources.

30. Haffenden, *Novelists in Interview,* 249.

31. Nancy E. Batty, "The Art of Suspense: Rushdie's 1001 (Mid-) Nights," *Ariel* 18, no. 3 (1987): 56–57.

32. Brennan, *Salman Rushdie and the Third World,* 103–109.

33. Parameswaran, "Handcuffed to History," 44.

34. Rushdie himself, presumably unintentionally, has shown himself to be an unreliable, or at best careless, narrator. On page 137 Dr. Schaapsteker is reported as having experimented with "the venom of the banded krait—*bungarus fasciatus*"; on page 147 he offers the family "diluted venene of the king cobra" as a last-resort kill-or-cure treatment for Saleem's typhoid, and Dr. Aziz administers "the cobra poison"; on page 153 Saleem reports: "Typhoid attacked me; krait poison cured me."

35. Keith Wilson, *"Midnight's Children* and Reader Responsibility," *Critical Quarterly* 26 (1984): 25–26.

Chapter Five

1. Fraser's Flashman novels include *Flashman, Royal Flash, Flash for Freedom, Flashman at the Charge, Flashman at the Great Game, Flashman's Lady, Flashman and the Dragon,* and *Flashman and the Redskins.* In *Flashman* (1969) the protagonist becomes involved in the first Afghan war (1839) and in *Flashman at the Great Game* (1975) in the Indian Mutiny (1857–58).

2. Haffenden, *Novelists in Interview,* 241.

3. Sura Prasad Rath, "Narrative Design in Salman Rushdie's *Shame," Journal of Indian Writing in English* 13, no. 2 (1985): 31.

4. Brennan, *Salman Rushdie and the Third World,* 119–21.

5. Brennan, *Salman Rushdie and the Third World,* 125.

6. That Rushdie has acknowledged that the girl in the second of these incidents is his sister (Haffenden, *Novelists in Interview,* 256) merely confirms a personal quality to these memories and reflections that is obvious from the text.

7. M. H. Abrams, *A Glossary of Literary Terms,* 5th ed. (Fort Worth: Holt, Rinehart & Winston, 1985), 135. Abrams maintains that only an "unsophisticated reader" will "identify the speaker with the poet himself" in "the lyric poems of Wordsworth and Keats." But when he proceeds to argue that "the 'I' in Wordsworth's 'We Are Seven' is not identical with that of the 'Intimations' ode, and neither of these with the speaker of his 'Ode to Duty,' " it is not clear to this reader how much such a statement differs from one to the effect that the Wordsworth who wrote "We are Seven" was not identical with the one who wrote

the "Intimations" ode, any more than either of those was identical with the one who wrote "Ode to Duty." In the strictest sense we can no more meet the same person twice than step in the same river twice, though we often speak as if we can.

    8. Salman Rushdie, "The Indian Writer in England," in *The Eye of the Beholder,* ed. Maggie Butcher (London: Commonwealth Institute, 1983), 76–77.

    9. One rupee equals approximately six cents at present exchange rates.

Chapter Six

    1. Rushdie, "Interview," *Kunapipi,* 26 (ellipses in the original).

    2. *The Satanic Verses* (New York: Viking Penguin, 1989), 6–7 (hereafter cited in text as *S.V.*). The N pagination is identical to that of the 1988 London edition.

    3. "A *chamcha* is a very humble, everyday object. It is, in fact, a spoon. The word is Urdu; and it also has a second meaning. Colloquially, a *chamcha* is a person who sucks up to powerful people, a yes-man, a sycophant. The British Empire would not have lasted a week without such collaborators among its colonized peoples. You could say that the Raj grew fat by being spoon-fed." Salman Rushdie, "The Empire Writes Back with a Vengeance," *Times,* 3 July 1982, 8. Hence: "Like Zeenat Vakil, Gibreel had reacted with mirth to Saladin's abbreviated name. 'Bhai, wow. I'm tickled, truly. Tickled pink. So if you are an English *chamcha* these days, let it be. Mr Sally Spoon. It will be our little joke.' " Note also what follows: "Gibreel Farishta had a way of failing to notice when he made people angry. *Spoon, Spoono, my old Chumch*: Saladin hated them all. But could do nothing. Except hate" (*S.V.,* 83).

    4. Salman Rushdie, in an interview with Sean French, *Observer,* 25 September 1988, reprinted in *The Rushdie File,* 7.

    5. Quoted by Michael T. Kaufman, from an interview with Salman Rushdie, *New York Times Book Review,* 3 November 1983, 23.

    6. Ruthven, *A Satanic Affair,* 41.

    7. Cf. Matt. 7:24–27.

    8. See Gen. 21:1–21, and compare with Gen. 22:1–13. For a different view of the latter incident, see the author's "Isaac and Iphigenia," in *Flying Dutchmen* (Victoria, B.C.: Sono Nis Press, 1983), 22–23.

    9. Salman Rushdie, "Open Letter to Rajiv Gandhi," reprinted in *The Rushdie File,* 36.

    10. Salman Rushdie, "Interview by Bandung File," printed in *The Rushdie File,* 22.

    11. Ruthven, *A Satanic Affair,* 55; see also note 15, chapter 2, above.

    12. See *Midnight's Children,* 82.

    13. See note 17, chapter 2, above.

    14. Milan Kundera, *The Art of the Novel,* tr. Linda Asher (New York: Grove Press, 1986), 7.

    15. Historically Salman al Farisi, a barber of Persian birth, was not one of

Muhammad's scribes, though he was a follower and did, as recounted in *The Satanic Verses,* advise the Prophet to build a defensive ditch around Medina. Nevertheless, there is a story told by Tabari, one of the two early Muslim commentators who record the story of the satanic verses, of a scribe who temporarily lost his faith when a mistake he made in transcription went unnoticed. See Ruthven, *A Satanic Affair,* 39.

16. Ruthven, *A Satanic Affair,* 47–48.

17. Rushdie, "*Midnight's Children* and *Shame,*" 3.

18. Talveen, the woman hijacker who eventually blows up the plane, uses very similar wording as she reveals the explosives attached to her naked body: "History asks us: what manner of cause are we? Are we uncompromising, absolute, strong, or will we show ourselves to be timeservers, who compromise, trim, and yield?" (81). Presumably we are to see, in her idea, one that is "smashed to bits."

19. Salman Rushdie, "The Book Burning," *New York Review of Books* 33, no. 3 (2 March 1989): 26, and Salman Rushdie, "Choice between Light and Dark," *Observer,* 22 January 1989, the latter reprinted in *The Rushdie File,* 61–62.

20. Hanif Kureishi, "Erotic Politicians and Mullahs," *Granta* 17 (1985): 144–45, and Ruthven, *A Satanic Affair,* 44–46. These two accounts differ somewhat, the latter acknowledging as its source Akbar S. Ahmed, "Death in Islam: The Hawkes Bay Case," *Man: Journal of the Royal Anthropological Institute* 21 (1986): 121–34.

21. Rushdie, "*Midnight's Children* and *Shame,*" 2.

22. Similar shifts elsewhere are sometimes "acknowledged" merely by the first-person words being set in italics.

23. Cf. "As flies to wanton boys, are we to the gods;/They kill us for their sport" (*King Lear,* act 4, sc. 1, lines 36–37).

24. The quotation "Why should the Devil have all the good tunes?" is attributed to Charles Wesley in *Brewer's Dictionary of Phrase and Fable,* centenary ed., rev., ed. Ivor H. Evans (New York: Harper & Row, 1981), 328.

25. Ruthven, *A Satanic Affair,* 41.

26. Ruthven, *A Satanic Affair,* 18, and D. J. Enright, "So, and Not So," *New York Review of Books* 36, no. 3 (1989): 25–26.

27. Rushdie has acknowledged much of what is said in the preceding four paragraphs in James Fenton's "Keeping Up with Salman Rushdie," *New York Review of Books* 38, no. 6 (1991): 26–34.

28. Brennan, *Salman Rushdie and the Third World,* 148.

29. *Times,* 2 May 1983, 10 and 1 November 1984, 16.

30. *Granta* 11 (1983): 123–41; *Observer,* 1 April 1984, 8.

31. *Azraeel* is the name Muslims and Jews give to the Angel of Death; here it is transferred to the trumpet on which he will sound the last trump.

32. Enright, "So, and Not So," 25.

33. *The Rushdie File,* 36.

34. Salman Rushdie, *In Good Faith* (New York: Viking Penguin, 1990), 4.

35. Such paintings are not a fictional invention. See Salman Rushdie, "Minority Literatures in a Multi-Cultural Society," in *Displaced Persons,* ed. Kirsten Holst Petersen and Anna Rutherford (Sidney, Australia: Dangaroo Press, 1988), 35.

36. *Grimus,* 135, and Haffenden, *Novelists in Interview,* 239.

Chapter Seven

1. Rushdie, "Interview," *Kunapipi,* 20.

2. Chinua Achebe, *Hopes and Impediments: Selected Essays 1965–87* (London: Heinemann, 1988), 18–19.

3. Rushdie, *In Good Faith,* 12.

4. *Times,* 3 July 1982, 8.

5. See James Harrison, "Mill and Darwin: The Natural Selection of Ideas," *Mill News Letter* 14, no. 2 (1979): 17–20.

6. Rushdie, *In Good Faith,* 6–7 (author's emphasis).

Selected Bibliography

PRIMARY WORKS

Books

Grimus. New York: The Overlook Press, 1979.
Haroun and the Sea of Stories. London: Granta Books, in association with Penguin Books, 1990.
Imaginary Homelands: Essays and Criticism. London: Granta, 1991.
In Good Faith. New York: Granta, 1990.
Is Nothing Sacred? New York: Granta, 1990.
The Jaguar Smile: A Nicaraguan Journey. London: Pan Books, 1987.
Midnight's Children. New York: Alfred A. Knopf, 1981.
The Satanic Verses. London: Penguin, 1988. Pagination identical to reprint, New York: Viking Penguin, 1989.
Shame. New York: Vintage International, 1989. Pagination identical to original edition, New York: Alfred A. Knopf, 1983.

Short Stories

"The Free Radio." *Atlantic* (June 1983): 23–25.
"The Golden Bough." *Granta* 7 (1983): 249–51.
"The Prophet's Hair." *Atlantic* (June 1981): 23–29.
"Yorick." *Encounter* 59 (September–October 1982): 3–8.

Articles

"After Indira, an Awakening or the Whirlwind?" *Times,* 1 November 1984, 16.
"The Book Burning." *New York Review of Books* 33, no. 3 (2 March 1989): 26.
"The Council Housing that Kills." *Guardian,* 3 December 1984, 12.
"Eating the Eggs of Love." *Granta* 20 (1986): 57–69; included as chapter 7 in *The Jaguar Smile*.
"Elias Canetti." *Listener* 106 (3 December 1981): 678–79.
"The Empire Writes Back with a Vengeance." *Times,* 3 July 1982, 8.
"An End to the Nightmare." *Independent,* 19 August 1988, 21.
"Exemplary Lives." *Times Literary Suplement,* 7 August 1981, 910.
"Fictions Are Lies that Tell the Truth." *Listener* (27 June 1985): 14–15.
"The Indian Writer in England." In *The Eye of the Beholder,* edited by Maggie Butcher, 75–83. London: Commonwealth Institute, 1983.

"Magnificient Obsession." *Observer Magazine,* 26 May 1983, 10–12.

"Midnight's Real Children." *Guardian,* 17 January 1987, 19.

"Minority Literatures in a Multi-Cultural Society." In *Displaced Persons,* edited by Kirsten Holst Petersen and Anna Rutherford. Sidney, Australia: Dangaroo Press, 1988.

"The New Empire within Britain." *New Society* (9 December 1982): 417–20.

"On Günter Grass." *Granta* 15 (1985): 180–85.

"Outside the Whale." *Granta* 11 (1983): 123–41.

"A Pen against the Sword: In Good Faith." *Newsweek,* 12 February 1990, 52–57. (Reprinted, with additions, as *In Good Faith.*)

"The Raj Revival." *Observer,* 1 April 1984, 19.

"Shame about the Pirates." *Times,* 24 November 1984, 8.

"She [Margaret Thatcher] Has Persuaded the Nation That Everything Which Goes Wrong Is an Act of God." *Guardian,* 23 May 1983, 9.

"Truth Retreats When the Saint Goes Marching In: *Gandhi.*" *Times,* 2 May 1983, 10.

"The War Widow Pressing for Peace." *Guardian,* 17 January 1987, 19.

SECONDARY WORKS

Books

Appignanesi, Lisa, and Sara Maitland, eds. *The Rushdie File.* Syracuse: Syracuse University Press, 1990. An invaluable collection of documents, interviews, and opinions on the whole *Satanic Verses* affair.

Ashcroft, Bill, Gareth Griffiths, and Helen Tiffin. *The Empire Writes Back: Theory and Practice in Post-Colonial Literatures.* London: Routledge, 1989. Little specifically on Rushdie, but good on the postcolonial background.

Brennan, Timothy. *Salman Rushdie and the Third World.* London: Macmillan, 1989. The first full-length literary study of Rushdie. Hurried—some inaccuracies and misreadings. Places him well in relation to third-world writing.

Rodinson, Maxime. *Muhammad.* Translated by Anne Carter from the French. New York: Pantheon Books, 1980. Classic biographical study of Muhammad by distinguished French scholar who lived and worked for many years in the Middle East.

Ruthven, Malise. *Islam in the World.* New York: Oxford University Press, 1984. A very readable account of the historical background and present state of Islam by a well-versed, sympathetic, but clear-sighted outsider.

Ruthven, Malise. *A Satanic Affair: Salman Rushdie and the Rage of Islam.* London: Chatto & Windus, 1990. Although clearly put together in haste, this study is a thorough and sympathetic account of both sides to the political and religious aspects to the Rushdie affair. Comments on the literary qualities of the novel are also shrewd and apropos.

Said, Edward W. *Orientalism.* New York: Vintage Books, 1979. Classic study of the Orient and Orientals as seen by Europeans and North Americans.

Articles

Batty, Nancy E. "The Art of Suspense: Rushdie's 1001 (Mid-)Nights." *Ariel* 18, no. 3 (1987): 49–65. Ingenious and illuminating technical examination of narrative strategies in *Midnight's Children.*

Cronin, Richard. "The Indian English Novel: *Kim* and *Midnight's Children.*" *Modern Fiction Studies* 33, no. 2 (1987): 201–13. A thoughtful attempt to see both *Kim* and *Midnight's Children* as fantasies, the former a rather better-constructed one.

Edmundson, Mark. "Prophet of a New Postmodernism: The Greater Challenge of Salman Rushdie." *Harper's,* December 1989, 62–71. *The Satanic Verses* seen as post-postmodernism and as offering a positive vision.

Parameswaran, Uma. "Handcuffed to History: Salman Rushdie's Art." *Ariel* 14, no. 4 (1983): 34–45. An early and still valuable survey of Rushdie's writing up to *Midnight's Children.*

Sangari, Kumkum. "The Politics of the Possible: The Narrative Modes of Gabriel Garcia Marquez and Salman Rushdie." *Cultural Critique,* no. 7 (1987): 157–86. Links *Midnight's Children* to a much fuller study of Garcia Marquez's output.

Wilson, Keith. "*Midnight's Children* and Reader Responsibility." *Critical Quarterly* 26 (1984): 25–26. Still one of the shrewdest comments on *Midnight's Children.*

Interviews

Contemporary Authors, vol. 3, 1984, 414–17.

Durix, Jean Pierre. *Kunapipi* 4, no. 2 (1982): 17–26.

Fenton, James. "Keeping Up with Salman Rushdie, *New York Review of Books* 38, no. 6 (1991): 26–34. Selected conversations with Rushdie linked by Fenton's comments and concluding with a review of *Haroun and the Sea of Stories.* Fascinating, moving, illuminating.

Haffenden, John, ed. *Novelists in Interview,* 231–61. London: Methuen, 1985. By far the most informative of the pre-*Satanic Verses* interviews.

Kaufman, Michael T. *New York Times Book Review,* 3 November 1983, 22–23.

Marzorati, Gerald. *New York Times Magazine,* 4 November 1990, 30–33, 68, 78, 84–85. The fullest account of Rushdie's life in hiding.

Newsweek, 12 February 1990, 47–51. Sheds light on Rushdie's recent life.

Index

The Author

James Harrison is a professor in the Department of English at the University of Guelph in Ontario. Born in Sri Lanka, he was educated in South India and England where, after helping to keep postwar Austria and Italy occupied, he studied English at Durham University. After teaching at a variety of schools and colleges in England, he parlayed a grossly overgrown M.A. thesis on "The Idea of Evolution in Nineteenth-Century Poetry" into an M.Litt. at Durham, emigrated to Canada, and accepted a position at the University of Guelph, where he has taught for twenty years.

Professor Harrison has published two volumes of poetry, one in England and one in Canada, and has two poems in the *Norton Introduction to Literature*. He has edited an anthology of scientific writing and has published articles in the *Journal of the History of Ideas, Philological Quarterly,* the *University of Toronto Quarterly,* and elsewhere, mainly on nineteenth-century literature and the history of ideas. He also wrote the Twayne volume on Kipling, which led to undergraduate and graduate courses on novels about India, an article on Rushdie, and this present volume.

Professor Harrison is married, has four children and two stepchildren, and lives in Toronto.